ISSUES THAT CONCERN YOU

Body Image

Heidi Williams, *Book Editor*

GREENHAVEN PRESS
A part of Gale, Cengage Learning

GALE
CENGAGE Learning™

Detroit • New York • San Francisco • New Haven, Conn • Waterville, Maine • London

Christine Nasso, *Publisher*
Elizabeth Des Chenes, *Managing Editor*

For more information, contact:
Greenhaven Press
27500 Drake Rd.
Farmington Hills, MI 48331-3535
Or you can visit our Internet site at http://gale.cengage.com

For product information and technology assistance, contact us at

Gale Customer Support, 1-800-877-4253
For permission to use material from this text or product, submit all requests online at
www.cengage.com/permissions

Further permissions questions can be emailed to permissionrequest@cengage.com

Articles in Greenhaven Press anthologies are often edited for length to meet page requirements. In addition, original titles of these works are changed to clearly present the main thesis and to explicitly indicate the author's opinion. Every effort is made to ensure that Greenhaven Press accurately reflects the original intent of the authors. Every effort has been made to trace the owners of copyrighted material.

Cover image copyright Benis Arapovic, 2008. Used under license from Shutterstock.com

LIBRARY OF CONGRESS CATALOGING-IN-PUBLICATION DATA

Body image / Heidi Williams, book editor.
   p. cm. — (Issues that concern you)
  Includes bibliographical references and index.
  ISBN 978-0-7377-4182-7 (hardcover)
  1. Body image in adolescence. I. Williams, Heidi.
  BF724.3.B55B64 2009
  306.4'613—dc22

                                            2008026756

Printed in the United States of America
2 3 4 5 6 7 12 11 10 09 08

CONTENTS

Most people would like to change *something* about their bodies and the way that they look, but for some people it is an obsession. A freckle, a mole, the size of their nose, the symmetry of their ears, the size of their breasts, whatever the flaw or flaws, major or minor, real or misperceived, noticeable or not, they are life consuming for people with body dysmorphic disorder (BDD).

Sufferers of BDD may refuse to have their picture taken, stop going out with friends, quit going to school, stop going to work, refuse to leave home altogether, and even attempt suicide. They may have multiple plastic surgeries or just spend literally hours a day looking at, trying to cover up, measuring, and thinking about their perceived defect. No amount of reassurance will comfort them.

Body integrity identity disorder (BIID) is a unique type of BDD. Sometimes called "amputee wannabees," sufferers feel that they will not be themselves until a certain limb or limbs are amputated. Driven to desperation, some have taken it upon themselves to remove their own limbs or have damaged them by freezing them so that they have to be amputated. Once the limbs are gone, they feel whole.

While people with BIID are desperate to remove something, others feel compelled, or just want, to add something. Body modification can range from the tame to the extreme. Multiple tattoos, multiple piercings, and piercings in every part of the body imaginable are becoming more common and more culturally acceptable. Some people go to greater extremes with things like tattoos covering their entire bodies, sewing beads into their skin, branding (burning a permanent scar), eyeball tattooing, eyeball jewelry, tooth filing, tongue splitting, ear pointing or shaping, and 3-D body modification such as horn implanting.

Some body alterations, like tattoos, are culturally acceptable in today's society.

Stalking Cat, often called the Catman, was born Dennis Avner. His list of body modifications includes tattooing, implants and silicone injections in his face so he can wear whiskers, other implants to make his face look more catlike, teeth filing, ear pointing, and upper lip splitting.

Where does normal stop and abnormal begin? Is there a normal? Ancient Mayans flattened infants' foreheads to make them prettier. In parts of China foot binding was practiced for almost a thousand years. For ages some cultures have valued stretched earlobes and necks. Not so long ago women permanently modified their waistlines and ribcages with corsets. Native American by birth, Stalking Cat began transforming himself after a native chief told him to "follow the ways of the tiger." On his Web site he explains that transforming oneself into one's totem is ancient Huron Native American tradition.

Some forms of body modification are completely acceptable in the current culture. Teeth straightening and whitening can cost thousands of dollars. Chemically coloring, straightening, or curling hair can be expensive and subjects everyone

Some people believe that spray tanning is a healthier way to achieve a tan than lying in the sun.

involved to breathing in harsh chemicals. Male circumcision is painful to infants and has little if any medical value. Plastic surgery requiring anesthesia involves risking death but is more and more acceptable and popular, even among teens.

Body image is something that impacts everyone's daily lives, whether in extreme ways, like those who have BDD, or in more subtle ways. The authors in this anthology explore a variety of issues related to body image. In addition, the volume contains several appendixes to help the reader understand and explore the topic, including a thorough bibliography and a list of organizations to contact for further information. The appendix titled "What You Should Know About Body Image" offers facts related to body image, as well as information about common disorders associated with body image. The appendix "What You Should Do About Body Image" offers tips on maintaining a positive body image and provides suggestions for raising awareness in the community. With all these features, *Issues That Concern You: Body Image* is an excellent resource both for researchers and for those concerned with their own body image.

ONE

Body Image Is an Issue That Concerns Most Teenagers

Karen Fanning

> Karen Fanning is a contributing writer for *Junior Scholastic*, a newsmagazine for the classroom, designed to engage middle school students. In this article Fanning discusses the struggle that teens have with body image. Using the words of teens and school counselors, she assures readers that feeling unaccepted by peers is more common than most realize. She also quotes National Football League (NFL) quarterback Matt Leinart, who as a child and teen was cruelly teased by his classmates because his eyes would cross and he was overweight. Fanning concludes with coping techniques for students, such as forming positive friendships or, as Leinart did, finding something at which they excel.

Last spring [2006], Cagney Cooper was walking out of gym class when a boy she barely knew approached her. He had a question. "He asked me if I was pregnant," says the 13-year-old from St. Louis, Missouri. "I'm not the skinniest of all people. I felt embarrassed."

Cagney is not alone. Most teens wrestle with feelings of insecurity and doubt. Caught between childhood and adulthood,

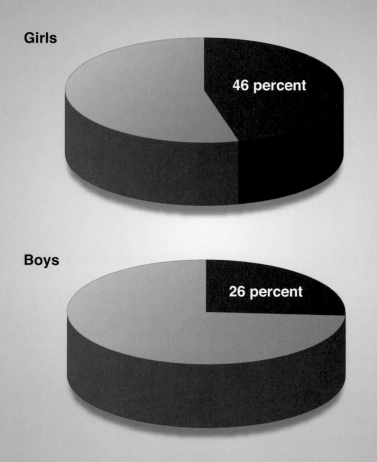

Percentage of Youth Reporting that They Are Significantly Distressed About Their Body Size and Shape

Girls

46 percent

Boys

26 percent

Taken from: Dianne Neumark Sztainer, Mary Story, Peter J. Hannan, Cheryl L. Perry, Lori M. Irving, "Weight-Related Concerns and Behaviors Among Overweight and Nonoverweight Adolescents: Implications for Preventing Weight-Related Disorders," *Archives of Pediatric Adolescent Medicine*, February 2002. http//:archpedi.ama-assn.org/cgi/content/full/156/2/171#ACK.

they feel awkward in their own bodies. For kids, the teen years can be a very bumpy ride.

Feeling Accepted

Adolescence is filled with uncertainty. "[Teens'] bodies are changing, their relationship with their parents is changing, their relationships with friends are changing," says Annie Fox, author of *Too Stressed to Think*. "On top of that, they aren't sure where they fit in, and fitting in means everything."

Anything that makes teens stand out—a few extra pounds, their parents' divorce, a learning disability—adds to their stress. As kids begin to become independent of their parents, fitting in with peers becomes increasingly important.

"Your friends are the new set of people you identify with," says psychologist Susan Bartell. "You become much more sensitive to what they think—whether they approve of what you are wearing, how you talk, who you are friends with, or how athletic you are."

From the class clown to the class president, teens want to be accepted. Some will do almost anything to win approval, even if that means bullying a classmate, experimenting with drugs, or slacking off in class.

"I try hard in school, but I hide it because my classmates make me feel bad," says Edgar Gomez, 13, of Ontario, California. "They'll say, 'You're the most annoying person. You think you know everything.' So I don't always do the best I can."

"The Whole Dorky Look"

National Football League (NFL) quarterback Matt Leinart hardly seems the ugly-duckling type. Recently, he signed a multimillion-dollar contract with the Arizona Cardinals. But the Heisman trophy winner from the University of Southern California was once a typically insecure teen. "I had the whole dorky look going," says Leinart, now 23 [as of 2006]. "I was a fat kid, and I'd get made fun of. When I didn't have my glasses on and I was tired, my eyes would cross, so everyone made fun of that too. Kids are so cruel to each other."

For Leinart, the answer was finding an activity he loved. "I turned to sports," he says. In the end, his early experiences gave him more confidence.

"It was a really tough time," Leinart told *Sports Illustrated* about his adolescence. "I got teased a fair amount. Maybe that's why I don't get upset these days when somebody says I'm overrated or

The Girls in Motion program uses nutrition and exercise to encourage girls to develop a healthy body image as they move into their teens.

that some other guy is better than me. Hey, they might be right. All I know is that I'm going to keep going out there and giving my best effort."

Like Leinart, many teens find that achieving something on their own can be better than fitting in. In any case, finding inner strength may require separating yourself from people who criticize you. This could even mean your friends, says Fox.

"Take a look at the people you call friends," Fox advises. . . . "Can you trust them or do they talk behind your back? Do they treat you with respect or do they put you down?" A true friend will stand by you.

Coping with Insecurity

How can *you* cope with insecurity? First, try being "your own best friend," says Celeste Chappuis, who counsels adolescents at Logos School in St. Louis, Missouri.

"Teens say things to themselves they would never say to anyone else," says Chappuis. "'You're fat, you're stupid, you're such a loser.' Become aware of what you say to yourself. It's a habit."

Next, realize that you're not alone. "You think you're the only one who feels the way you feel—ugly, too big, too small," Chappuis [says]. "You think you're the only one who's ever been left out. But everyone is feeling the same way you are."

Even bullies. Cagney figures that the boy who teased her probably has his own insecurities. "I think he may have some problems, so if he puts other people down, it makes him feel better about himself," she says. "I'm able to stick up for myself. I'm a good person. I stay positive."

TWO

Body Image Is an Issue That Concerns Males

Nancy Clark

Nancy Clark is a nutrition consultant to competitive athletes and author of two books on sports nutrition. She is writing here for *American Fitness* magazine, which is published by the Aerobics and Fitness Association of America, the world's largest fitness educator. In this article, she says that body image is not just a women's issue. The rise in the portrayal of bare-chested, muscular men on TV and in print ads is directly affecting how men are viewing their own bodies. In some cases, men develop muscle dysmorphia and take extreme measures to develop muscle, like drinking multiple protein shakes a day, exercising excessively, and taking steroids.

Muscle dysmorphia is a new syndrome emerging behind gym doors. You might notice it in your gym's weight room. Some weightlifters pathologically believe their muscles are too small. They have poor body image (i.e., are ashamed of, embarrassed by and unhappy with their bodies) and a passionate desire to not only build muscle, but also avoid gaining fat. This preoccupation with building muscles manifests itself in excessive weightlifting (e.g., spending four or more hours per day at the gym), attention to diet (e.g., consuming protein shakes on a rigid schedule), time spent "body-checking" (e.g., looking in mirrors, CDs, window reflections, etc.), excessively weighing themselves (i.e., 10 to 20 times per day), too little time spent with family and friends and, not uncommonly, anabolic steroid use.

Men Idealize Big Muscles

Is this overconcern with body size a new obsession? Perhaps. In the past few years, we have been increasingly exposed to half-naked, muscular male bodies (e.g., Calvin Klein underwear ads). Evidently,

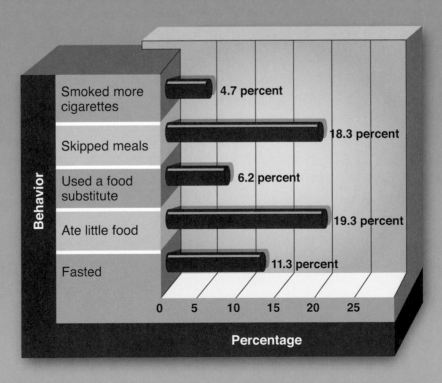

Percentage of Adolescent Boys with Unhealthy Weight Loss Behaviors

Taken from: Dianne Neumark Sztainer, Mary Story, Peter J. Hannan, Cheryl L. Perry, Lori M. Irving, "Weight-Related Concerns and Behaviors Among Overweight and Nonoverweight Adolescents: Implications for Preventing Weight-Related Disorders," *Archives of Pediatric Adolescent Medicine*, February 2002. http//:archpedi.ama-assn.org/cgi/content/full/156/2/171#ACK.

even brief exposure to these images can affect a man's view of his body. In a study of the media's effect on male body image, a group of college men viewed advertisements featuring muscular men, while another group viewed neutral advertisements without partially naked male bodies. Then, the men (unaware of the hypothesis being tested) were given a body image assessment. Those exposed to the muscular images showed a significantly greater discrepancy between the body they ideally want to have and their current body size. Another study suggests up to a third of teenage boys are trying to gain weight to be stronger, fitter, attain a better body image and perform better in sports.

Women Are Not Looking for Big Muscles

The irony is while college-age men believe a larger physique is more attractive to the opposite sex, women report desiring a normal-sized body. In a study of men from the United States, Austria and France, the subjects were shown a spectrum of body images and asked to choose:

- the body they felt represented their own
- the body they would ideally like to have
- the body of an average man their age and
- the male body they felt women preferred

The men chose an ideal male body that was about 28 pounds more muscular than their current bodies. They also reported believing women prefer a male body with 30 pounds more muscle than they currently possessed. Yet, an accompanying study indicated women actually preferred an ordinary male body without added muscle.

Teens Define Themselves by Their Bodies

At the 2003 Massachusetts Eating Disorders Association's (MEDA) annual conference, Dr. Roberto Olivardia shared his research on adolescent boys' body image. Olivardia is a psychology instructor at Harvard Medical School and co-author of *The Adonis Complex: The Secret Crisis of Male Body Obsession*. The title alludes to Adonis, the Greek god who exemplifies ideal masculine beauty and desire of all women. Olivardia explained that adolescence is a time for exploring "Who am I?" Without a doubt, so much of who a teen is, is defined by his body. Because today's boys have been exposed from day one to GI Joe action figures, Hulk Hogan and Nintendo's Duke Nukem, they have relentlessly received strong messages that muscular bodies are desirable. Those at risk for muscle dysmorphia include adolescent boys who were teased as children about being too fat or short. Individuals at highest risk are those who base their self-esteem solely on their appearance.

In our society, muscularity is commonly associated with masculinity. According to Olivardia, compared to ordinary men, muscular men tend to command more respect and are deemed more powerful, threatening and sexually virile. Muscular men perceive others as "backing off" and "taking them seriously." Not surprisingly, men's desire for muscles has manifested itself in a dramatic increase in muscle (and penile) implants.

The Danger of Steroids

Olivardia expressed concern the "bigger is better" mindset can often lead to anabolic steroid use. He cited statistics from a study with 3,400 high school male seniors: 6.6 percent reported having used steroids; more than two-thirds of that group started before age 16. Olivardia regrets males commonly use steroids in secrecy and shame. "Men will tell someone they use cocaine before they admit to using 'juice' [steroids]." This commonly keeps them from seeking help.

Steroids carry with them serious medical concerns: breast enlargement, impotence, acne, mood swings, risk of heart disease, prostate cancer, liver damage and AIDS (from sharing needles)—not to mention sudden death, although it may occur 20 years from current use. "Roid rage," the fierce temper that contributes to brutal murders and violence against women, is an immediate danger.

What's the solution? According to Olivardia, young men need education about realistic body size to correct the distorted thought "if some muscle is good, then more must be better." They might also need treatment for obsessive-compulsive disorder. Sadly, most men believe they are the only ones with this problem

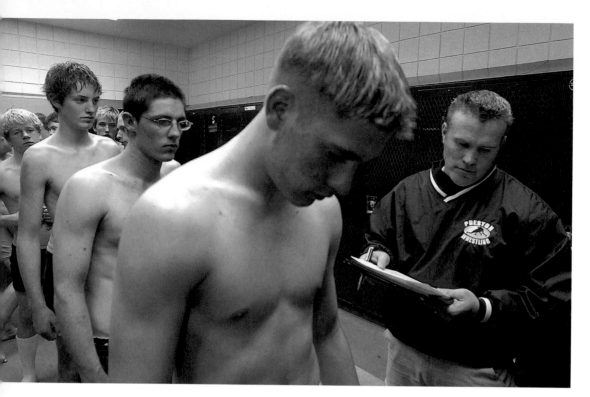

Unhealthy weight-loss practices are often associated with wrestling. Many states have set standards for the amount of weight teen wrestlers can lose.

and, thereby, take a long time to admit needing therapy. When they do, too few programs exist to help them explore the function this obsession serves in their lives—a sense of control. They mistakenly believe control over their bodies equates to control over their lives.

If you are a male struggling with dysmorphia, read *The Adonis Complex: The Secret Crisis of Male Body Obsession* and other books available [on the topic]. A Web search on "muscle dysmorphia" can also yield hundreds of articles with helpful information. Most importantly, know you are not alone—seek help and find peace.

THREE

Body Image Is an Issue That Concerns African Americans and Other Minorities

Amanda Dawkins

Associated Press writer Amanda Dawkins examines the prevalence of eating disorders among African Americans and other minorities. She explains that in the past, research and stereotypes have suggested that eating disorders are a middle- and upper-class phenomenon, with cases rarely presenting themselves in minority and low-income women. More current research, however, breaks those stereotypes. While new research shows that eating disorders are indeed increasing among these populations, researchers are also noting that in the past these populations were underrepresented in the research. Reasons for the increased prevalence in diverse communities may include a desire of second-generation Asians to blend in with their American friends and the zeal of educators trying to combat high obesity rates in Hispanic and African American communities.

The common perception is that eating disorders afflict only white women, especially upper- and middle-class women. While those are the most reported cases, specialists believe all socio-economic and ethnic groups are at risk.

For Liza LeGrand, it all started with anorexia in her early 20s, self-starvation that later included episodes of gorging on food and purging. At 5-feet-2, she got down to 70 pounds. LeGrand is Puerto Rican and dealing with what many believe is a "white woman's" problem.

The Stereotype

"For so long there was the belief that eating disorders only involved young white women," said Gayle Brooks, a black psychologist specializing in eating disorders at the Renfrew Center in south Florida where LeGrand was treated. "What they saw were exclusively white women with the problem."

Black and Hispanic women were thought to be less likely to develop anorexia and bulimia because more voluptuous physiques are generally considered attractive within their ethnic groups. A study in the *Journal of Counseling in Psychology* in 2001 found that African-Americans were more accepting of larger body shapes and less concerned with dieting.

Margaret Garner, nutrition director at the University of Alabama's medical center in Tuscaloosa, said this view was expressed frankly in a graduate class in health. In the past 25 years, she has counseled only one black woman with an eating disorder. She asked her class why the number of reported cases among black women was so low.

"An African-American male student readily said that he thought the reason there were no black females with this problem is that black men preferred some meat on the bones of their girlfriends and white men preferred them boney," Garner said.

But Laurie Mintz, an associate professor of counseling psychology at the University of Missouri–Columbia, said adoption of "Western values concerning attractiveness and thinness may increase minority women's risk for the development of eating disorders."

Research over the last decade has found these eating disorders among minority women and lower-income women, she said. Increasingly, anorexia and bulimia may be becoming "an equal opportunity disorder," Mintz said, citing other researchers.

Many churches are now promoting physical fitness to members who have been overlooked by the fitness industry. These women exercise to gospel music.

The Lack of Research

According to the National Eating Disorders Association, there are no reliable statistics on the prevalence of eating disorders among minorities, but diverse communities are underrepresented in the research.

Brooks suggested several reasons for the invisibility of minority women suffering from eating disorders:

- Because minority and poor women don't fit the profile, doctors and therapists often fail to assess them properly for eating disorders.
- Education efforts haven't been directed toward ethnic groups, so family and friends often miss the early signs.
- For some poor women, it may be hard to get adequate treatment.

Stephen Thomas, director of the Center for Minority Health at the University of Pittsburgh, says he has met only one African-American with anorexia.

"Other than the color of her skin, she matched her middle-class white counterparts when it came to the important factors associated with the disease," he said.

He is concerned that these eating problems may increase as health agencies target overweight minorities. Two-thirds of Americans are overweight or obese, and the percentages are higher among blacks and Hispanics.

"As the nation becomes focused on obesity as a national obsession, we must be aware of unintended consequences," said Thomas. "We do not want to create conditions to contribute to eating disorders in our zeal to address obesity."

Mintz also says complex cultural issues must be weighed in considering risks to different ethnic groups.

"In other words, the complex issues that may result in an eating disorder in a 15-year-old middle-class white girl, such as pressures to be thin, struggles with independence, may be different than the complex issues that may result in an eating disorder in a second-generation 15-year-old Korean-American girl," who may want to separate from her parents and eat more "American" like her friends.

The longer eating disorder sufferers go without treatment, Brooks says, the more it could become a chronic problem leading to death.

One Woman's Experience

LeGrand knows how life-threatening it can be. The 36-year-old Orlando, Fla., resident was hospitalized for a month in 1998 because of the damage her purging did to her body. While she has been admitted into two treatment centers in the past, she continues her struggles with her disorder.

The first time LeGrand was admitted to a treatment center was while she was attending a university in Michigan.

"The dean somehow found out and they called my parents and told them," LeGrand says.

She says she felt betrayed and her experience at the first clinic did not go well.

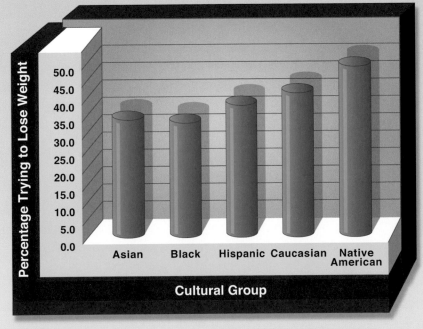

Body Image Is an Issue for Young People of All Races

Of more than six thousand young people interviewed, similar percentages of each cultural group reported attempting to lose weight, with the exception of Native Americans, who reported a higher rate.

Taken from: M. Kilpatrick, C. Ohannessian, and J. Bartholomew, "Adolescent Weight Management and Perceptions: An Analysis of the National Longitudinal Study of Adolescent Health," *Journal of School Health*, April 1999.

A patient at the Renfrew Center in Florida in 2001 and 2002, she says her treatment there has been helpful. Now a mother, LeGrand is currently on disability because she has diabetes along with the eating disorder.

She said she did not binge or purge during her pregnancy and for a few months after out of concern for her child, but she eventually returned to the behavior she has tried so hard to put behind her.

"There are moments, of course. Everyone has their days, but now I know how to control it," she says. "I'm a lot stronger."

FOUR

Body Image Is Not an Issue That Concerns African American Women

Dakota Smith

> This article, written by Dakota Smith for the Inter Press Service, appeared in Women's e News, a nonprofit, independent news service covering issues of importance to women. In it Smith examines the results of two recent studies that reveal new information about the issue of body image among African American women. One study found that African American women seldom compare themselves with or experience negative body image while watching thin, white women on television, the way many white women do. Another study repeated these findings but also found that African American women are negatively affected by watching African American models, but only if the subjects experience poor self-esteem. Overall, African American women felt better about their bodies, perhaps because they idealize a more realistic body weight and because they tend to define beauty by such concepts as style rather than by weight.

Turn on the television or flip through a fashion magazine and you're likely to face one predominant image: a white, thin, pretty woman.

Eating Disorders Among Black and White Women

Percentage of Black and White Women

Black | White

Anorexia Nervosa: Black 0.0, White 1.5
Bulimia Nervosa: Black 0.4, White 2.3
Binge-Eating Disorder: Black 1.4, White 2.7

Eating Disorder

Taken from: http://mchb.hrsa.gov/whusa04/pages/ch2.htm.

If studies have long shown that white women are negatively influenced by seeing size 0 and 2 women in the media, how do black women react to similar images?

Two new studies examining media's role in influencing body image conclude that black women pay little attention to images of thin, white women. They also seem to suggest that black women have better body images than white women, despite being heavier, and perhaps, unhealthier than their white counterparts.

Prime-Time Reactions

The first study, conducted by the University of Michigan and published in the [June 2004] issue of *Psychology of Women Quarterly*, looked at popular television's influence on black women.

Researchers quizzed black and white female college students at the University of Michigan about their reactions to such popular television shows as "Beverly Hills 90210," "Frasier," "Friends," "Martin" and "Sister, Sister."

The researchers found that even though only 5.6 percent of the characters on prime-time television are black women, those black women who were studied were mostly unscathed by watching numerous hours of television programs featuring thin, white women.

"Basically, black women just don't feel bad in the same way white women do by watching television," says L. Monique Ward, professor of psychology at University of Michigan and one of the four authors of the study, *Who's That Girl: Television's Role in the Body Image Development of Young White and Black Women.*

On the other hand, white women were more likely to compare themselves to the women they saw on television and more likely to have more negative thoughts about their body.

But black women shrugged off the ideal of the thin, pretty white woman as "unattainable for themselves and as unimportant to others in the black community," according to the authors.

Fewer Eating Disorders

Overall, both the black women and the white women who participated in the University of Michigan study had the same body types.

Despite weighing about the same, the black women in the study were less likely than white women to exhibit signs of bulimia.

The study found that white women were more likely than black women to agree with statements like "I eat moderately in front of others and stuff myself when I am alone" and "I am preoccupied with a desire to be thinner."

The authors concluded that part of the reason black women felt better than whites, was that black actresses on popular television shows tend to have more realistic body types.

Mikki Taylor, beauty director at *Essence* magazine, isn't surprised by the study's findings. She believes that black women's identification with black characters on television—and rejection of the media images—confirms the wide range of ideals of beauty among black culture.

"There just isn't a black standard of beauty to live up to," she says. "We celebrate our uniqueness, whether it's different skin hues, or different hair. Unlike mainstream culture, there is no one standard that is going to make us feel inferior."

And when blacks watch television, "there's not a yearning on the part of the audience to look like any other culture," she adds.

Wanting Beyoncé's Body

A Missouri School of Journalism study published in the *Journal of Black Studies* in March 2004 studied the effects that magazine advertisements—featuring attractive images of white and black young women—played in shaping the self-image of black women.

The study showed magazine advertisements to black college students at the University of Missouri. Like the participants in the Michigan study, black women dismissed images of attractive white women as unimportant. But when shown images of attractive black women—with both curvy and thin bodies—black women with low self-esteem were negatively affected.

"They weren't affected by pictures of a white Victoria Secret model for instance, but images of Tyra Banks made them feel bad," says Cynthia Frisby, assistant professor of journalism at the University of Missouri, who conducted the study. Tyra Banks is an African American supermodel.

The women who felt relatively good about their bodies were not negatively influenced by images of idealized black beauty, according to Frisby.

Overall, Frisby found that the majority of black women in her study reported favoring having heavier and hippier bodies, figures more like singer Beyoncé Knowles. And for the most part, they were closer to that ideal than that of the ideal of the thin white women.

"Black women are a lot more confident about their bodies, even if they are overweight," says Frisby. "Much of it is cultural, with black men preferring women with bigger hips and bigger butts."

Indeed, the researchers at Michigan also found that the notions of beauty for black women were different from those of white women. The researchers reported that the black women in their study defined beauty based on traits such as style, movement and character, rather than weight and appearance.

Either way, the body types seen on television and in magazines hardly represent the average female population, even if some

Some African American women define beauty by characteristics such as style, rather than by weight.

television shows and magazine advertisements feature black women with heavier bodies.

A report released earlier this year [2004] by the American Heart Association found that 77 percent of black women are overweight, compared to 57 percent of white women.

Body Confidence Debated

Despite the studies' findings, not everyone agrees that black women are more confident about their bodies than white women.

"So we don't aspire to be waif-like, blond-haired, blue-eyed women," says Janette Robinson-Flint, director of the Los Angeles-based Black Women for Wellness, a grassroots organization dedicated to promoting the health and well-being of black women. "But I do think as black women, we work hard to come to terms with our bodies."

She argues that even if television portrays blacks with more realistic body types, in real life black women are judged by more criteria than white women, for instance, whether their hair is straight or the relative lightness or darkness of their skin color.

In addition, she believes it's a misconception that the majority of black women don't feel a pressure to be thin. "It's something I hear black women talk about everyday," she says.

She also notes that while a bigger body may be celebrated in black culture, black women are also facing greater health risks, such as heart disease, than white women.

University of Missouri's Frisby agrees that black women need to pay more attention to a healthy diet and exercise. In her next study, she says she will examine the role of black women and health problems such as heart disease and breast cancer.

"As a culture, we're not concerned about our weight, but we need to be," she says.

FIVE

The Media Are to Blame for Poor Body Image in Teenagers

Fiona Bawdon

In *New Statesman*, a British current events magazine, Fiona Bawdon, a legal journalist, reports on the connection between images of unrealistically thin women in the media and the high rate of body dissatisfaction and eating disorders in girls and women. Recent studies have established a direct link between the two and also underline the growing prevalence of eating disorders, especially among younger women. Suggestions for a solution to this problem include protection for models, including unionization and medical exams, as well as requiring a health warning on photos retouched to make models look thinner or healthier.

As London Fashion Week sashayed to a close on 20 September [2007], most of the media coverage was of the clothes, rather than the skeletal frames of the girls inside them. Yet the week coincided with the publication of recommendations from a controversial inquiry into the health of fashion models, set up after two Latin American models died from eating disorders, one after collapsing on the catwalk.

In her report, the chair of the Model Health Inquiry, Baroness Kingsmill, said she had found "startling" evidence of the vulnerability of models, who are at "high risk" of eating disorders. The inquiry heard evidence from an editor who said she'd sat through "innumerable shows where I have been unable to take in the clothes through shock at the emaciated frames of models". A writer said the fashion world was "numb", looking at models only as "clothes hangers" and "failing to see whether they are healthy or not". The inquiry made 14 recommendations to improve the

The Council of Fashion Designers of America contributed to a health initiative to help models avoid eating disorders following criticism of the overly thin appearance of many runway models.

working lives of models, including banning under-16s [girls 15 and younger] from the catwalk and introducing compulsory medical checks and a trade union.

The importance of the report, however, is not just that it reveals exploitation of young women in the fashion industry. There is now a whole body of evidence that links fashion and media images directly to the health and well-being of the wider population of teenage girls.

In a study of 3,200 young women carried out in February this year [2007] by Girlguiding UK, over half of 16- to 25-year-olds said the media made them feel that "being pretty and thin" was the "most important thing". A quarter of girls aged between ten and 15 said the same. The most influential role models by far (cited by 95 per cent of girls) were Kate Moss and Victoria Beckham, both of whom are famously thin. In another study—*Sex, Drugs, Alcohol and Young People*, by the Independent Advisory Group on Sexual Health and HIV, published in June [2007]—nearly 30 per cent of 11-year-old girls expressed dissatisfaction with their body weight, and one in ten was on a diet. By age 15, 46 per cent of girls were unhappy with their weight, and a quarter of them were dieting.

Eating Disorders Are Becoming More Prevalent

Professionals working in this field are convinced that the number of teenage girls with an eating disorder is going up, and that sufferers are getting younger. The majority are aged 14–25, but girls as young as eight have been diagnosed. The last reliable survey into eating disorders across Britain dates back to 1990, but in Scotland, where new research was conducted in 2006, there had been a 40 per cent increase since 1990.

Teenage girls say they are influenced by pictures of impossibly skinny women, even when they don't want to be. At a recent conference in London about teenagers and the media, organised by the campaign group Women in Journalism, one teenager encapsulated the views of many of the 50 or so girls present, saying the fashion to be super-skinny made her "feel really ugly. I know it's really stupid but I still follow it. It makes me feel really insecure."

This young woman's experience is all too common, according to Professor Janet Treasure, director of the eating disorders unit at the South London and Maudsley NHS Trust, who has conducted research into the impact of the "size zero culture". She says looking at pictures of thin women reduces self-esteem—and adolescents are among the most susceptible to these pressures. Adolescents are also the group most likely to suffer long-term ill-effects from eating disorders because their bodies are still developing.

Susan Ringwood, chief executive of beat, the eating disorders charity, gave evidence to the inquiry. She supports its conclusions, but says restricting its remit to protecting young women in the modelling industry, rather than tackling the impact of "size zero" culture on the wider population, was an opportunity missed.

The Role of Media

Ringwood accepts that it's a gross oversimplification to blame the rise in eating disorders entirely on the media's focus on thinness and dieting, but says it does play a part. "Eating disorder sufferers say: 'How come it's OK for celebrities to look like that and not me? How come they're being celebrated on the front of a magazine and I'm in hospital being told I'm going to die?'"

Although the Model Health Inquiry acknowledged this is an area outside its remit, it included a recommendation for a code of conduct to govern the digital manipulation of photos. The inquiry heard evidence of retouching to make models look thinner or even to make ill models look well—something of great concern to those working with eating disorder sufferers. "These processes add pressure to models to meet an unattainable ideal," it said. One suggestion was for retouched photos to carry a "health warning" so that the reader knows what she's looking at isn't real. The teenagers at the London conference were previously unaware that magazine images are routinely airbrushed: thighs slimmed, wrinkles smoothed and blemishes removed.

Of course, media coverage of skinny women is far from universally positive. But even critical coverage of celebrities who are deemed to be "too thin" can make matters worse for eating disorder sufferers, according to Ringwood. Low self-esteem is a recognised factor: sufferers don't think they are worthy of taking up any space in the world, and shrink accordingly. Seeing bodies that look similar to theirs being pilloried and described as revolting reinforces their own lack of self-worth, she says.

Bodies Beautiful

Ringwood acknowledges that the causes of eating disorders are many and complex; they include factors such as genetic disposition and personality type, often compounded by traumatic events—for instance, bereavement or bullying. "But the final piece of the jigsaw is the social context," she says. Add the media, which celebrate impossibly skinny bodies over all other types, and numbers of sufferers are bound to increase. She would welcome a move for magazines to specify when images have been retouched.

It is a view shared by many of the sufferers themselves. Asked what was the one thing that would help prevent such conditions, most sufferers said it would be for the media to show more "real" bodies. They ranked this as more important than greater understanding from parents, or even greater medical knowledge. "Why can't the media promote healthy, normal-sized people?" lamented one typical respondent.

Ringwood says the media and the fashion industry should present a more diverse mix of body types as beautiful and acceptable. Such a change would not be a total solution by any means, but it would help, she argues. "We can't change brain chemistry and we can't protect young women from all forms of trauma. Of all the factors involved in eating disorders, images in the media are the one area we can change."

SIX

The Media Are Embracing More Diverse Body Types

Barbara Lippert

Barbara Lippert has appeared on CBS and CNN as an advertisement commentator and is a columnist for *Adweek* magazine, the source of this article. In it she describes the current popular trend toward the acceptance of less-than-perfect bodies in the media, particularly on television, citing examples like the hit show *Ugly Betty*, Dove soap's "Campaign for Real Beauty," and the cancellation of the show *Extreme Makeover*. This trend toward the acceptance of average people seems to be a backlash from the media's obsession with perfection. Looking at the bigger picture, however, Lippert sees this trend as nothing more than a trend, and a shallow one at that.

ABC's *Ugly Betty* is a show with a mean-spirited title and a seemingly well-worn premise: Place a slightly overweight, badly dressed young woman with glasses and braces on the staff of an excruciatingly snobby women's fashion magazine, and watch the designer fur fly.

But unlike all the editorial assistants/Cinderellas before her—most notably, the one in *The Devil Wears Prada*—Betty (America Ferrera) has not, as of yet, stripped off the glasses and gotten beautiful. Yes, she has trimmed her Marx Bros.-level eyebrows, but otherwise sticks with her signature look: polyester separates set off by fiercely gleaming orthodontia. That's because the show is not about whether Betty will ditch the poncho or get Da Vinci tooth veneers. Rather, what resonates is her humanity, intelligence and authenticity in the face of her mean, superficial workplace family. *Ugly Betty* has become a breakout hit because it upends standard cliches about woman and beauty and, along the way, forces us to reconsider the notion of what is ugly and what is beautiful—and, while we're at it, what is ethical and what is real.

More Authentic Stars

A rejection of inauthenticity is not being limited to the make-believe world of TV. Personalities are coming under scrutiny as well, as seen by the negative reaction to [television personality] Star Jones when she refused to come clean about her stomach

Overweight Characters on Television Sitcoms and Dramas

Year	Character	Show	Actor
1964	The Skipper	*Gilligan's Island*	Alan Hale, Jr.
1964	Pugsley Addams	*The Addams Family*	Ken Weatherwax
1982	Norm Peterson	*Cheers*	George Wendt
1988	Roseanne Conner	*Roseanne*	Roseanne Barr
1991	Newman	*Seinfeld*	Wayne Knight
1995	Drew Carey	*The Drew Carey Show*	Drew Carey
1999	Tony Soprano	*The Sopranos*	James Gandolfini
2000	Sookie St. James	*Gilmore Girls*	Melissa McCarthy
2003	Berta	*Two and a Half Men*	Conchata Ferrell
2004	Turtle	*Entourage*	Jerry Ferrara
2004	Hugo 'Hurley' Reyes	*Lost*	Jorge Garcia
2005	Kirstie Alley	*Fat Actress*	Kirstie Alley
2005	Phyllis Lapin	*The Office*	Phyllis Smith

[Compiled by the book editor]

bypass surgery (no doubt one reason she was booted from *The View*). And Jenny Craigster [actress] Kirstie Alley, by no means model thin, was cheered for the 75 pounds she has very publically lost; the audience was also more than forgiving about her choreographed bikini reveal on *Oprah*. With the recent death of a young Brazilian model from complications of anorexia, we're also witnessing a waif backlash, to which the worldwide fashion industry has responded by imposing and/or considering weight minimums for their runway models. Another sign of the time: famously anti–cosmetic surgery actress Diane Keaton now appears in L'Oreal ads via [advertising agency] McCann Erickson.

A Reaction to Obsession

Enough is enough, it would seem in more than just politics. In fact, welcome to the comfort and authenticity of an *Ugly Betty* moment, a much-needed cultural correction from the obsession with cosmetic perfection. It's fueled, in part, by the inevitable re-action to any extreme trend. . . . Having a nightmare plastic surgery story to tell (after her scarred, not-ready-for-the-red-carpet breast implants were posted all over the Internet) has actually helped B-list actress Tara Reid get herself booked on talk shows recently.

An air of desperation and fear resonates from the unmoving foreheads and giant lips plastered in magazines and on TV. And that says much about Hollywood's tossing aside of anyone over 35—and how this emphasis on youth and perfection trickles down to the culture at large. Which brings us to the baby boomers. Blame it on exhaustion, but one could argue that they have approached the age where they either need to give in to and/or embrace the aging process, or go broke (and, possibly, physically harm themselves) trying to stave it off.

A Return to Normal

What is clear is that, from a pop culture standpoint, the pendulum has swung back to the middle. *Extreme Makeover*, for instance, devoted to giving people the cosmetic surgeries of their dreams, was yanked off the air after one episode this season due to low ratings. Spinoff *Extreme Makeover: Home Edition* has become a mainstay. The big difference: *Home Edition* focuses not on the self-obsessed, but on truly needy people—the kind who bring multiple-disabled foster children into their homes or who themselves have suffered terrible health problems or losses.

Proving that more-attainable types of beauty are officially in vogue, *Entertainment Tonight* jumped on the compassion bandwagon for mid-November sweeps when correspondent Vanessa Minnillo did a heavily promoted hidden-camera investigative series entitled "Ugly Vanessa." The former beauty queen spent hours on the street encased in fake fat to see whether she'd be treated differently. She was. She got ignored or was made fun of—reactions quite different to the overwhelmingly positive attention she received in her other investigative outfit—a blonde wig and miniskirt. The searing insight that people generally prefer hot blondes in miniskirts to fat people allowed her to make a final ringing statement about the need for sensitivity for the overweight.

"Real Beauty"

With its "Campaign for Real Beauty" from [advertising agency] Ogilvy & Mather, Dove has worked steadily on a more genuine and authentic stance for women. This fall [2006], Dove's latest move was an Internet video, "Evolution," which asks, "How did our perception of beauty get so distorted?" Then, in sped-up time, it shows an average-looking woman sitting through 10 hours of hair and makeup. Yet to meet "model" standards, she still has to have her neck lengthened and her eyes enlarged (courtesy of airbrushing and Photoshop) before the image can be put on a billboard. The video has gotten some 500,000 hits on YouTube plus thousands of girls and women posted their appreciative feelings about it on the Dove Web site.

Another brand, L'Oreal, has decided to embrace instead of eradicate the wrinkle by using Keaton, an actress who famously refuses to go under the knife. "I want to express my age and be authentic," she was quoted as saying in regard to the ad. "Why do so many people follow somebody else's idea of what's attractive?"

Model Rachel Hunter lost ten pounds in ten weeks for her role as spokesperson for Slim-Fast's "Find Your Slim" campaign promoting the idea that no one ideal weight or size suits everyone.

Stars Speak Out

Keaton, along with [actresses] Jamie Lee Curtis and Cybill Shepherd, also spoke out against cosmetic surgery recently on *Access Hollywood*. Shepherd told the camera that she likes her boobs just the way they are: "They're more flexible this way. I can wear them up or down." And Jane Fonda, who has had more public cycles than a Maytag washer—she was anti-cosmetic surgery in the '70s and then face-lifted in the '80s—is again in step with the Zeitgeist [spirit of the times], announcing that she is off plastic surgery (no better living through plastics).

It shouldn't surprise us that even those who can afford it—least of all Fonda, given her past political agendas—are putting aside the pursuit of physical perfection. We're bombarded with images from Iraq, Darfur and, closer to home, post-Katrina New Orleans—images unavoidable in this era of YouTube.

The new media provide outlets to express the pangs of social conscience and common decency that are the natural reactions to public ugliness. Certainly, this was the case for shutting down Judith Regan's Fox TV interview with O.J. Simpson to coincide with the publication of his book, *If I Did It*. The idea so repulsed advertisers and the public that Rupert Murdoch apologized and announced that it was being pulled.

Media Could Still Do Better

But this rejection of perfection is hardly a revolution. While we're in the throes of celebrating regular folks—the sweat and tears of the teams on CBS's *The Amazing Race*, the multi-cultural, all-shapes-and-sizes (but sweaty) talent on Bravo's *Top Chef*—it is vastly overpowered by the overwhelming consensus that thin is in and aging an embarrassment to be overcome. Yes, *Entertainment Tonight*'s Minnillo put on a fat suit, but it turned out to be more of a celebration of her thin, pretty self.

And Americans, to borrow a term from *New York Times* writer and former Botox addict Alex Kuzcynski, are still beauty junkies. (Her well-received book, *Beauty Junkies: Inside Our $15 Billion Obsession with Plastic Surgery*, was published [in 2006].) Botox use is exponentially on the rise and, according to the American

Society for Aesthetic Plastic Surgery, since 1997 there has been an increase of 444 percent in the total number of cosmetic procedures. (The percentage has remained relatively constant over the last few years, however, for teens 18 and younger.)

And given that *Ugly Betty* is on network TV, how long could it possibly take before the curvy Latina character gets her nips and tucks?

It looks like at least a season. The storylines are following her love life and her family as she also finds career success—despite the polyester. As Ferrera told the gals on *The View* about her character, "It's not about looking ugly. It's just about looking past what you see. Achieving that image is not all you were put on this planet to do. On the show, you get to watch the other people blossom into real human beings because Betty reminds them what it is to be real." And maybe the show also offers a return to baseline normal, where natural has to be good enough because we have more important things to do.

SEVEN

Heredity Is to Blame for Body Image Disorders

Sarah Karnasiewicz

Sarah Karnasiewicz, deputy editor of *Salon*, a daily online magazine, reports on doctors' new theories on the causes of anorexia. Past theory has maintained that anorexia is primarily caused by factors in a person's environment such as stress, peer pressure, or exposure to images of unhealthily thin stars in the media. Recent theories, however, propose that while certain environments may trigger anorexia, genetics and brain chemistry lay the foundation for it, not unlike depression and alcoholism. Consequently, anorexia —or rather a predisposition to anorexia—also can be passed on through lineage.

If everything you know about anorexia comes from Lifetime movies and high school health class, you might want to check out this week's *Newsweek* [December 2005] cover story.

In "Fighting Anorexia: No One to Blame," reporter Peg Tyre debunks many common assumptions about the disease, starting with the stereotype that it afflicts only overachieving, wealthy, white girls. In fact, Tyre tells readers, in the past decade doctors have encountered an increasingly diverse population of patients, including blacks, Hispanics, Asians and boys, from preadolescence to middle age.

Sarah Karnasiewicz, "A New Look at Anorexia," *Salon*, December 1, 2005. This article first appeared in *Salon* at www.salon.com. An online version remains in the *Salon* archives. Reprinted with permission.

Anorexia in Children

Most disturbing are Tyre's accounts of child anorexics like Matthew Cornwell, who, at age 9, starved himself down to 39 pounds by limiting his daily caloric intake to one carrot topped by a tablespoon of peanut butter. Or 10-year-old Katherine Krudys, whose parents begged, pleaded and even promised to buy her a pony if she'd eat, but still stuck to "portions that could be measured in tablespoons." In the end, both of their downward spirals ended in emergency room visits—and extended stays in eating-disorder treatment centers.

Indeed, anorexia, while always debilitating, can wreak particularly brutal harm on children's bodies. Tyre explains, "While adults can drift along in a state of semistarvation for years . . . in the preteen years, kids should be gaining weight"—weight they need to foster bone and muscle growth, strengthen their hearts and brains, and lay down the new neurological "pathways" that are an essential component to adolescent growth spurts.

A Dangerous Disease

No matter the age, anorexia is a serious—indeed deadly—battle, a chronic condition that can be treated but rarely cured. The statistics Tyre shares are not encouraging: "About half of anorexics get better," she writes. "About 10 percent of them die. The rest remain chronically ill—exhausting, then bankrupting, parents, retreating from jobs and school, alienating friends as they struggle to manage the symptoms of their condition." Some doctors believe "anorexics use starvation as a mode of self-medication," Tyre reports, since by "eating less, anorexics reduce the serotonin activity in their brains . . . creating a sense of calm, even as they are about to die of malnutrition. . . . It has the highest mortality rate of any mental illness, including depression."

New Theories

The parallels to depression are worth noting, and are the key to understanding some of doctors' new theories about the source of the disease. As Tyre writes, for years "conventional wisdom [has] held that adolescent girls 'got' anorexia from the culture they

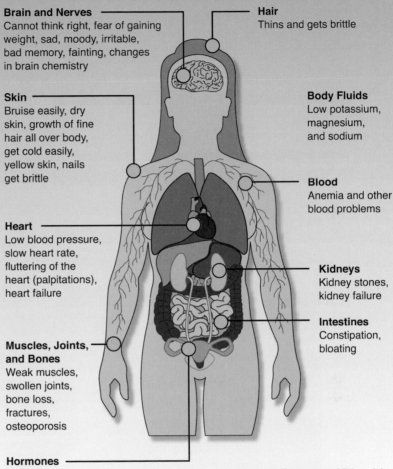

Anorexia Affects Your Whole Body

Brain and Nerves
Cannot think right, fear of gaining weight, sad, moody, irritable, bad memory, fainting, changes in brain chemistry

Hair
Thins and gets brittle

Skin
Bruise easily, dry skin, growth of fine hair all over body, get cold easily, yellow skin, nails get brittle

Body Fluids
Low potassium, magnesium, and sodium

Blood
Anemia and other blood problems

Heart
Low blood pressure, slow heart rate, fluttering of the heart (palpitations), heart failure

Kidneys
Kidney stones, kidney failure

Intestines
Constipation, bloating

Muscles, Joints, and Bones
Weak muscles, swollen joints, bone loss, fractures, osteoporosis

Hormones
Periods stop, problems growing, trouble getting pregnant. If pregnant, higher risk of miscarriage, having a C-section, baby with low birthweight, and postpartum depression.

Taken from: http://womenshealth.gov/faq/Easyread/anorexia-etr.htm. Office on Women's Health in the U.S. Department of Health and Human Services.

lived in," specifically from unrealistic body images presented in the popular media. Now doctors have begun to equate anorexia to other afflictions like alcoholism and depression—diseases "that may be set off by environmental factors such as stress or trauma, but have their roots in a complex combination of genes and brain chemistry."

"In other words," Tyre writes, "many kids are affected by pressure-cooker school environments and a culture of thinness promoted by magazines and music videos, but most of them don't secretly scrape their dinner into the garbage." Adds Cynthia Bulik, director of the eating-disorder program at the University of North Carolina at Chapel Hill, "The environment 'pulls the trigger' . . . but it's a child's latent vulnerabilities that 'load the gun.'"

Parents can help form a young person's body image.

New Fears

This new theory has both absolved parents of stigma and exposed them to new fears, since while poor parenting may not [be] the cause of their child's suffering, genes very well may be. For Amy Nelson, 14, the realization that her disease might be hardwired came when her father recovered a diary kept by his younger sister, who died of "unknown causes" in 1980. In it the young woman chronicled her attempt to lose 13 pounds in a month by keeping her diet to 600 calories a day. "No salt, no butter, no sugar, 'not too many bananas,'" the woman had written in her journal.

With that in mind, doctors now believe that a family-centered approach to therapy and treatment is the most humane and most effective way to rehabilitate youths with eating disorders. Regular family dinners—already touted for their power to prevent obesity, depression and drug addiction—are also heralded as the perfect opportunity for parents to model healthy nutrition to their families and keep track of children's eating habits.

The silver lining in Tyre's story is that progress, while fragile, is possible. Remember Katherine Krudys, who at 10 measured her meals in teaspoons? She's home now, in sixth grade, eating three meals a day—even baked potatoes with sour cream.

And she finally got that pony.

EIGHT

Positive Body Image Begins with Good Parenting

Amy Votava

> Amy Votava, a mother and fiction writer, wrote this article for *Mothering*, an independently owned magazine that emphasizes a natural family lifestyle. As the mother of a daughter, she has noticed the multitude of commercial products and visual media messages that define beauty by thinness and has wondered why so many people make a point to teach their children to accept all races and cultures but not all body sizes. She urges readers to examine their own prejudices and their own comments about weight, including how they talk about their own bodies. She also recommends talking openly with children, using images in the media as conversation starters about body sizes in the real world and the beauty of bodies of all sizes.

All I want to do is buy my prescription medication at the local drugstore. My five year old, Olivia, is holding my hand and walking next to me as we head toward the checkout counter. It should be an uneventful errand, but it isn't.

First we walk past the fashion magazines. Every cover features women who all look the same—white, in their 20s, very thin. I muse over headlines with such claims as "LOSE WEIGHT WITH THE MIRACLE SANDWICH" or "GET THINNER WITH THE NEW CHOCOLATE

Amy Votava, "Every Body is Beautiful: Teaching Children About Size Acceptance," *Mothering*, March 2004, pp. 41–43. Reproduced by permission.

DIET." Next comes a point-of-purchase display of the pharmacy's array of weight-related products. You name it, they sell it—cellulite cream, metabolism boosters, even a product that claims to have put "exercise in a bottle." I grit my teeth and silently wish I didn't have to see all these messages every time I fill my prescription. Then it hits me—*I'm not the only one seeing them.* I look down at Olivia, who is innocently singing a little song to herself and swinging my hand back and forth. My stomach lurches with double the force. The message being put forth to my daughter and me is this: A body with fat is a body with a problem.

In a well-known experiment, children were shown drawings of a variety of children. These drawings included a child of normal weight, a fat child, and children with various handicaps, including missing hands and disfigured faces. These children rated the fat child as the least likable. This bias also affected the larger children, who revealed the same prejudice. Children as young as six described a child with a fat silhouette as "lazy, dirty, stupid, ugly, cheats and lies."

Most of us strongly disapprove of our children making sweeping generalizations about particular racial, cultural, or religious groups, and we make efforts to educate our children about such matters. But we parents need to ask ourselves: When it comes to body size, do we make the same effort?

Teach Children About the Biology of Size

For children to begin to celebrate diversity in body size, they need to be informed that body size and shape are largely genetic matters. There is no doubt that we can choose our behaviors. We can choose to satisfy our appetites with healthy food, eating when we are hungry and stopping when we are full. We can choose to make exercise a part of our lives. But the body that results from these efforts is something we cannot choose.

Dr. Craig Johnson, director of the Eating Disorders Program at Laureate Psychiatric Clinic and Hospital, was recently answering questions on an Internet forum hosted by PBS. In part of his response to a depressed person's plea for a way to lose weight, he said: "The problem is that very few people have the genetic

The body as a deeply rooted physical expression of a person begins at a very early age and can be molded by a child's parents.

potential to be the size and shape idealized in our culture. That is the stone-cold harsh reality of genetically mediated weight and shape regulation. I make a point with my patients that I am 5' 10" tall. If I developed a belief system that I would only have self-esteem if I could become 6' 2" tall, I would be doomed to low self-esteem." We wouldn't tell a child that 2 plus 2 equals 15. Similarly, we should not be teaching children that *diet* plus *exercise* equals *thin*.

Here's a point where you can give yourself a refresher course as well. Don't you try to notice if you happen to have a racist thought? Do you evaluate and examine these thoughts? Do the same with thoughts that are size-biased. Do you find yourself assuming that the large person you just saw eats too much, is lazy, or both? If you are large, do you say these things to yourself? If you find yourself assuming that a fat person eats too much, remind yourself that this may not be true. Some people who are large—as well as some people who are thin— are compulsive eaters. Some are not. You simply can't know just by looking at someone.

If you homeschool your children, you can use *Healthy Body Image: Teaching Kids to Eat and Love Their Bodies Too!* by Kathy Kater. This curriculum is a series of lessons developed to empower third and fourth graders to form a foundation for the acceptance of various body types, based on recognizing what people can and can't control in regard to body size and shape. If you don't homeschool your children, call the school they attend and suggest that the school include this program, or something like it, in its syllabus.

Change Images in the Home

Many of us take great pains to fill our homes with racially diverse images. We make sure that we have books, posters, and dolls that reflect a wide range of cultures. This, we feel, will combat the constant lack of such images in the outside world. The same approach can apply to body size. Decorate your walls with images that depict all kinds of shapes. What a beautiful thing it would be to have the pleasing image of Diego Rivera's slender wife, Frida Kahlo, next to the equally pleasing brushstrokes that depict [Pierrre-August] Renoir's round, blonde bathers! A friend of mine commented that she always feels at ease in homes that have pictures of naked women of various size. She is not a large woman, but this kind of display of appreciation for the human form makes her feel comfortable. For our children, such ease could be a way of life.

Pay Attention to What You Say

When you look in the mirror, do you pat your stomach and grimace? Do you imply that you are happy because your pants feel loose? These actions are subtle, but they send powerful messages to our children. If your children see that you're unable to celebrate your body, how will they be able to celebrate the diversity in others' bodies? In their own bodies?

Encourage an open dialogue on the subject of body size. If your child happens to assume that a fat person you know is "lazy," it might be tempting to jump in and correct the child. However, this situation is also a great opportunity to ask questions such as, "Do you think that this person has fat parents, too?" or "Do you know anyone who is large but really loves to play sports?" These questions can be great instigators for learning.

Nancy Summer, a leader in the size-acceptance movement, actually invites children to insult her during the workshops she conducts with sixth graders. Nancy herself is very large, and the children hesitate to insult her. However, in one class a girl looked her in the eye and said "Horse!" Nancy asked the class to keep the animals coming. "Whale!" "Elephant!" they yelled. "Cow!" "Pig!" She joyfully wrote all of these animals down, then discussed with the class how beautiful these animals really were.

Talk to Your Children About the Media

The average American woman is 5 feet, 4 inches tall and weighs 142 pounds. When was the last time you saw a woman who looked like that on television, in a magazine, or on a billboard? When I first heard this statistic, I was shocked. But then I began to look around—at real everyday people on the street, at the grocery store, at the public pool. Not only did this exercise confirm for me that the average woman really is this size, it also opened my eyes to the actual diversity of the human body. I began to enjoy the many different shapes around me, like a beautiful canvas with unusual patterns—some angular, some soft and free-flowing and voluptuous, some perfectly round like a circle. Encourage your children to do the same, then have them compare what they see in the real world to what they see in the media. Do reality and image match up?

I recently interviewed a group of 40 fourth-grade children in a private school three weeks after they'd completed the *Healthy Body Image: Teaching Kids to Eat and Love Their Bodies Too!* curriculum. I showed them an advertisement from a magazine featuring three women modeling various clothing. I said to them, "I think this advertisement is a little boring. Do you have any idea why?" One boy blurted out, "Well, I think it's boring, too! All of those women look exactly the same. Their hair and their bodies are exactly the same!" A little girl interjected, "I think it might even be the same woman." Finally, another child said, "What exactly are they trying to sell me, anyway? I can't even tell."

Indeed, what are such advertisements trying to sell us? It's important for our children to know that what the advertisers are

Eating Disorder Triggers

A panel at the 2004 International Conference on Eating Disorders in Orlando, Florida, suggested the following spectrum of risk factors. The more triggers a person exhibits, the greater the probability of developing an eating disorder.

- High weight concerns before age 14
- High level of perceived stress
- Behavioral problems before age 14
- History of dieting
- Mother diets and is concerned about appearance
- Siblings diet and are concerned about appearance
- Peers diet and are concerned about appearance
- Negative self-evaluation
- Perfectionism
- No male friends
- Parental control
- Rivalry with one or more siblings
- Competitive with siblings' shape and/or appearance
- Shy and/or anxious
- Distressed by parental arguments
- Distressed by life events occurring in the year before the illness develops
- Critical comments from family members about weight, shape, and eating
- Teasing about weight, shape, and appearance

trying to sell is, primarily, the feeling that we are somehow lacking. They assume that if we feel lacking in some way, we will need to buy something to fix the problem. And one way to make us feel that we are lacking is by showing us images of people the majority of us do not match up to.

In that same interview, a little girl told me, "One day I saw an ad on television. It was really strange. There was a perfect family sitting around a perfect-looking kitchen. They were all gorgeous [thin] and laughing and having fun. Then, suddenly, cereal started raining from the ceiling and falling into their empty bowls. I really never figured out what the commercial was for. But I think that they were trying to tell me that if I bought what they were selling, my life would be perfect." This from a fourth grader. Children can grasp these things. We just need to get them started.

Although size acceptance is an issue of social justice, it hasn't gotten as much attention as other issues. Teachers tell me that in schools it is no longer acceptable to tease children about the color of their skin or the religion they practice. Fat children, on the other hand, are still teased, often openly, sometimes without intervention by adults. Accepting the natural diversity in the sizes and shapes of each others' bodies seems to be a last frontier of sorts. But, as is the case with many problematic aspects of our culture, if we educate our children, the problem can be reversed.

During the same interview with fourth graders, I told them about the experiment in which children shown pictures of many kinds of children picked the fat child as the least likable. "Now that you have had these lessons about body size," I asked, "what would you do if you had to pick the least likable child?" A multitude of hands shot up in the air, waving and bouncing. I called on a red-headed girl in the front. She said, "I would say, 'How can you expect me to do this when I have no idea who these people are on the inside?'" Thirty-nine other little heads nodded in unison.

NINE

Weight-Loss Surgery Is a Good Option for Many Obese Adolescents

Jeff Evans

Family Practice News is an independent newspaper that informs family physicians about developments in medicine and news relevant to the medical profession. In this article senior writer Jeff Evans argues that morbidly obese older children and teens are good candidates for weight-loss surgery. While it seems that young people may not be responsible enough to handle the restrictions imposed by such surgery, evidence suggests the opposite. To support his point Evans cites three studies in three different countries involving three different types of weight-loss surgeries. In every study the patients were as compliant and the outcomes as successful as those of adult patients.

Few morbidly obese adolescents are referred for bariatric surgery [weight-loss surgery], despite the high rate of failure with conservative interventions. But short-term outcomes and compliance in teens undergoing Roux-en-'Y gastric bypass' [RYGB, weight-loss surgery in which the stomach is stapled off into a large pouch], laparoscopic adjustable gastric banding [LAGB, weight-loss surgery in which a band is placed around the upper part of the stomach], or biliopancreatic diversion [BPD, a more complicated weight-loss surgery in which some of the stomach is removed, and parts of the intestines are bypassed] are as good as those of older patients, according to findings from a series of

After gastric bypass surgery, this teenager stays in shape through diet and exercise.

small retrospective studies presented at the annual meeting of the American Society for Bariatric Surgery.

The Common Objection

Those who object to doing bariatric surgery in adolescents question "whether teenagers will comply with the treatment regimen," said Dr. George A. Fielding of the surgical weight loss program at New York University, New York. "It's been postulated that kids won't do this just by the nature of being a teenager."

While in Dr. Fielding's care at the NYU Medical Center, 81 adolescents have received . . . LAGB. Five of the patients were aged 12–13 years, 55 were aged 14–17 years and 21 were aged 18–19 years. Most (60) were girls and weighed an average of 137 kg [302 lbs] with a mean [average] body mass index (BMI) of 48 kg.

Good Results in New York

After 1 year of follow-up in 32 patients, the patients lost 57% of their excess weight on average and had a mean BMI of 34. All comorbidities [illnesses caused by morbid obesity] were resolved, except for two patients who needed to maintain antidepressant therapy.

Banding adjustments at follow-up visits is a "key issue to the management of all LAGB patients, and it's no different with children," Dr. Fielding pointed out.

During the first year of follow-up in 27 patients aged 14–17 years, an average of 6.5 banding adjustments were made during 10 visits. This led to an average of 64% excess weight lost; only 2 of these 27 patients lost less than 50% of their excess weight, Dr. Fielding said.

Most patients reported that they were much less hungry and were eating a substantially smaller volume of food than they had been preoperatively. Very few had a desire to binge eat, he said.

The decision to undergo LAGB had been made mostly by the adolescents rather than by their parents, Dr. Fielding said. When performing LAGB in adolescents in Australia and in New York, he has taken a hands-off approach. "If you tell teenagers they can do pretty much what they like, they'll rear back in shock and usually do what you ask them to," he said.

Good Results in Brazil

In a separate report, Dr. Jose S. Pinheiro of the Hospital Sao Camilo, Sao Paulo, Brazil, reviewed his center's experience in performing laparoscopic [RYGB] surgery in 49 adolescents with a mean age of 16 years. The patients, 35 of whom were male, all received preoperative psychiatric evaluations and had full parental support. . . .

No patients died or had complications during surgery, and their average hospital stay was 30 hours.

The patients' mean BMI dropped from 45 before surgery to 23.5 at a mean follow-up of 48 months. All obesity-related co-morbidities resolved after surgery.

Dr. Pinheiro and his colleagues are still collecting quality of life data, but he said that all of the patients are happy with the surgery and are committed to becoming healthier. "The patients were extremely compliant with treatment," Dr. Pinheiro said, noting that all of them exercised on a regular basis. "Gastric bypass should be offered as an option in the treatment of obese adolescents," he added.

Good Results in Italy

When adolescents are referred for bariatric surgery, they are usually offered a restrictive procedure, said Dr. Francesco S. Papadia of the department of surgery at the University of Genoa (Italy). Malabsorptive [designed to interfere with the absorption of calories through the instestine] procedures, such as biliopancreatic BPD are "considered unsuitable . . . despite the lack of any evidence" against its safety or effectiveness in adolescents.

During 1976–2005, 76 adolescents received BPD surgery at the University of Genoa. Excluding 7 patients. . . , the remaining 68 had a mean of 11 years of follow-up, ranging from 2 to 23 years. On average, the patients were nearly 17 years of age at the time of the operation, weighed 125 kg [about 275 lbs] and had a BMI of 46. No patients died during surgery, and one had a wound dehiscene [rupture].

At their longest point of follow-up, patients lost a mean of 78% of their excess weight. Four patients lost less than 50% of excess weight. Of those, three underwent a revision and one was converted from a vertical banded gastroplasty with a preoperative BMI of 26.

Obesity-related comorbidities resolved in a significant percentage of patients; hypertension was reduced from 49% to 9%, dyslipidemia [a type of high cholesterol] from 16% to 0%, and glucose-intolerant or type 2 diabetes from 7% to 0%.

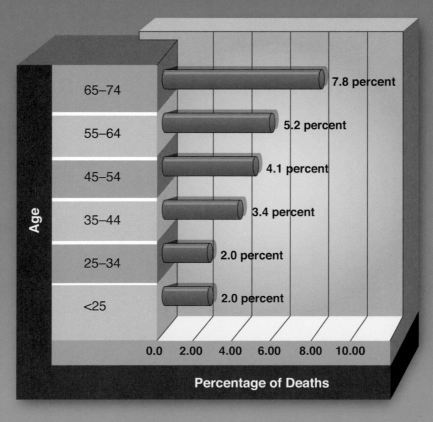

Bariatric Surgery Mortality Rates by Age After One Year

Age	Percentage of Deaths
65–74	7.8 percent
55–64	5.2 percent
45–54	4.1 percent
35–44	3.4 percent
25–34	2.0 percent
<25	2.0 percent

Taken from: *Journal of the American Medical Association.* http://jama.ama-assn.org/cgi/content/full/294/15/1903.

Twelve patients developed protein malnutrition at some point 1–10 years after surgery, and two patients had recurrent protein malnutrition. Those who experienced protein malnutrition after surgery had significantly higher initial body weight and BMI than did those who did not have malnutrition.

The incidence of protein malnutrition decreased steadily during the 30-year period of the study from 30% in the first few years to 2% in the last few years. The length of the common limb remained 50 cm, but as the surgeons gained experience, they adapted alimentary limb lengths [the length of the remaining digestive tract] to individual characteristics, and gastric sizes were not restricted to prevent protein malnutrition, Dr. Papadia said.

In a range of 4–18 years after BPD surgery, 18 women gave birth to 28 healthy infants. One infant was mentally retarded. Another two women died of severe protein malnutrition at the end of their pregnancies.

A total of 19 reoperations were performed in 14 patients, including 5 elongations and 2 restorations. Overall, three patients in the cohort died (4%)—two from protein malnutrition during pregnancy and one from acute pancreatitis.

TEN

Weight-Loss Surgery Is Not a Good Option for Most Obese Adolescents

Todd C. Frankel

Todd C. Frankel, a celebrated general assignment reporter for the *St. Louis Post-Dispatch*, discusses the special risks involved with weight-loss surgery in teens. With national coverage of successful postsurgery weight losses in some individuals, including teens, and with teen obesity rates at an all-time high, the demand for weight-loss surgery is only increasing. While some physicians believe that more teens and even preteens should qualify for surgery, many disagree. Risks include complications from the surgery itself and postsurgical problems such as severe malnutrition.

Morning again and Ashley Hardy was still in Room 524 at Cincinnati Children's Hospital. Yet another day in this strange city, some 500 miles from her North Carolina home, trying to figure out what was wrong.

Five months had passed since Ashley's weight-loss surgery in February 2004. Doctors thought she'd be in good spirits by now. But the 15-year-old with curly brown hair and a sweet, raspy voice lived in near-constant, unexplained pain. Only morphine made it bearable.

Ashley is one of a growing number of teens turning to weight-loss surgery. Despite all the attention paid to adults having the surgery, many doctors believe the future of the operation rests with teens. Teens stand to gain the most from an early intervention against the cruel medical and social realities of severe obesity, some doctors say.

Only a small number of adolescents—perhaps a few hundred—have tried the high-risk, radical surgery to lose weight. But that number is expected to grow rapidly as more hospitals offer the procedure.

At least 10 children's hospitals nationwide, plus an unknown number of surgery centers, perform the operation. More are expected [in 2005]. In Missouri, two hospitals—St. Louis Children's Hospital and the University of Missouri Children's Hospital in Columbia—are working to launch the state's first programs this year.

Greater Benefits, but Greater Risks

But if the benefits promise to be greater for young patients, so are the risks. Little is known about how teens fare after weight-loss surgery, and nothing is known about how they do decades out. One of the most comprehensive studies looked at just 33 patients. Concerns remain that these young people have given up too early on less drastic options. . . .

Ashley's mother had tried locking the kitchen cabinets and the refrigerator. Anything to keep Ashley, a compulsive eater, away from food. She was enrolled in intensive weight-management programs. She tried weight-loss camp. But it was always a tug of war. And Ashley was losing.

She weighed 385 pounds. She was excused from gym class because the exertion was too much. Her doctor told her she'd be dead by age 30 if she didn't lose weight.

Ashley's weight had been a problem since she was 5. It bothered her most late in elementary school. "I didn't have a group to fit into," Ashley said. "There were the little cheerleader girls, the ones who wore jeans and cute skirts and tops that I couldn't wear."

Amanda Munson is among two hundred teens taking part in a study on the safety of bariatric surgery on adolescents.

By the seventh grade, she began to find her own friends, "a group of oddballs," she said, despite her endless struggle with her weight.

In the summer of 2003, Ashley, then 14, saw an episode of the TV show "20/20," where two teens talked about the success of their weight-loss surgery. Ashley had just given up on another disappointing diet. She had been diagnosed with sleep apnea, a breathing condition caused by excessive weight. She was forced to wear a cumbersome oxygen mask to bed each night.

In December 2003, mother and daughter flew to Cincinnati for an evaluation. They chose Cincinnati Children's because it's a national leader in teen bariatric surgery. Once there, Ashley was given every manner of test, from a bone-density scan to an echo-cardiogram and psychological exam. They informed her of the risks.

Taking the Risk

She was approved and got a surgery date: Feb. 9, 2004. Ashley and her mother were excited.

The path that Ashley followed to surgery was detailed . . . July [2004] in the journal *Pediatrics*. Ashley's surgeon, Dr. Thomas Inge, was the lead author on the report.

The report described for the first time how hospitals should set up special centers to focus on childhood obesity with surgery as an option. Surgery would not be considered for girls younger than 13 and boys younger than 15. They needed to be much more overweight than adult patients. They must have completed at least six months of dieting, counseling and exercise. And if that failed, then surgery "may provide the only practical alternative for achieving a healthy weight and for escaping the devastating physical and psychological effects of obesity," the report says.

"The surgery is not for pudgy 9-year-olds," San Diego bariatric surgeon Dr. Alan Wittgrove said. "What we're talking about is kids who have serious medical problems just in that they are so overweight."

An estimated 255,000 adolescents in the United States are obese enough to be considered for surgery.

How It Works

At Cincinnati and most other pediatric hospitals, the operation of choice is the gastric bypass—a permanent procedure that reduces the stomach's size by 90 percent and bypasses a portion of the intestinal tract. Patients eat less with their smaller stomachs. They absorb less with their abbreviated intestinal tract.

"What you create is a tool by which portion control can be enforced," Inge said at a medical meeting in October [2004]. This is "significant negative reinforcement."

Reactions to the landmark report varied.

Some physicians, including Wittgrove, called for more aggressive surgery, including scrapping age limits and doing the surgery earlier.

Wittgrove, who estimated he has done the surgery on 75 adolescents, understands the reluctance to operate on patients so young. "But I think as you allow morbid obesity to go longer, you're going to hurt them," he said.

Even with age limits, the push to operate on teenagers is met with resistance, said Dr. Craig Albanese, who helped write the report.

Justifying the Risk Too Soon?

"How do you justify the risk in a kid? Well, you just turn it around," said Albanese, who last year launched a teen bariatric surgery program at Lucille Packard Children's Hospital in Palo Alto, Calif. "How do you justify the risk of not doing something?"

Others worry that teens are being pushed into surgery.

Gastric Bypass Surgery Complications: Fourteen-Year Follow-Up

Complication	Percentage
Vitamin B_{12} deficiency	39.9 percent
Readmit for various reasons	38.2 percent
Incisional hernia	23.9 percent
Depression	23.7 percent
Staple line failure	15.0 percent
Gastritis	13.2 percent
Cholecystitis	11.4 percent
Anastomotic problems	9.8 percent
Dehydration, malnutrition	5.8 percent
Dilated pouch	3.2 percent

Taken from: National Institutes of Health. Data derived from source (Pories WJ [595]) and modified based on personal communication. www.ncbi.nlm.nih.gov/books/bv.fcgi?rid=obesity.table.347.

Dr. Sarah Barlow at St. Louis University, who applauded the standards set by Cincinnati Children's, noted surgery is supposed to be a last resort. Yet good dietary and exercise plans have not been given sufficient attention or funding, said Barlow, a pediatric gastroenterologist specializing in childhood obesity.

The surgery costs $25,000 on average, Barlow noted. What if that money went instead to support high-quality weight-management programs?

"If no alternative programs are available, these adolescents have no real opportunity to attempt behavior-based weight management," she wrote in the journal *Pediatrics*. "To say the patients have failed is to place blame unfairly.". . .

Inge agrees that attempts at diet and exercise should come first, but he said in an e-mail interview that "extreme obesity" requires "extreme measures," including surgery. . . .

A Growing Demand

No one knows how many children are having the operation. The American Society for Bariatric Surgery offers detailed estimates for adult operations but not children and teens. Same for the International Bariatric Surgery Registry.

But doctors agree the number is growing amid increasing demand.

"I have been called by many families," said Dr. Tamir Keshen, a professor of surgery and pediatrics at Washington University in St. Louis who operates at St. Louis Children's.

Lee Fetter, president of St. Louis Children's, said a bariatric program was "in the early stages" with hope of starting later this year [2005].

Keshen said he planned to move ahead cautiously and rely on the expertise of adult bariatric surgeons at Barne-Jewish Hospital.

Plans for a similar teen program are in the works at the University of Missouri Children's Hospital in Columbia. Dr. J. Stephen Scott, a bariatric surgeon who for years worked in the St. Louis area, was recruited last summer [2004] to be the school's co-director of bariatric surgery. He is interested in operating on teens. "There is a significant need," Scott said.

The Problem of Noncompliance

Surgery is not the hard part for most patients. It is the constant attention to diet.

With smaller stomachs and shortened digestive tracts, patients need to make sure they get enough protein, vitamins and nutrients. The only way to do that is with pills.

Doctors try to impress upon patients, especially young ones, the importance of taking the pills. But it comes down to teens shouldering the responsibility.

"It's a tough thing to know if they really understand that," Scott said.

Sticking to a regimen like this is called compliance. Compliance is a known problem for teens who have diabetes or get organ transplants. A 1994 study of 34 teens who had bariatric surgery painted a bleak picture: Only 13 percent of the teens took their vitamin B12, multivitamins and calcium pills as instructed.

The problems can be serious. Cincinnati Children's doctors wrote a paper last year [2004] highlighting three cases of a disease called beriberi. Before gastric bypasses, beriberi was thought to have disappeared from developed countries. Caused by a lack of thiamin, or vitamin B1, it can lead to everything from arm and leg numbness to heart problems, brain problems and coma. Taking vitamins prevents it.

One teenage gastric-bypass patient described in the Cincinnati report suffered repeated falls, pain in her legs and fading hearing that confounded doctors until she was diagnosed with beriberi. It took some time, but she was able to walk again without help.

Inge, the Cincinnati surgeon, said he and his colleagues now discuss these possible problems with new and old patients.

Three days after her gastric bypass last February, Ashley Hardy left the hospital. She stayed in Cincinnati for a week at her doctor's request. She lost 32 pounds in six days and felt close to good.

Severe Complications

But by week's end she was throwing up. Ashley was rushed to the emergency room with a serious stomach pouch leak. Ashley and her mother stayed in Cincinnati until the middle of March. They only briefly returned home.

Ashley spent more than 90 days in hospitals in Charlotte, N.C. and Cincinnati through the end of the summer as she struggled with pain and nausea. She had several procedures to pry open her stomach's opening after it repeatedly swelled shut. Doctors offered a range of diagnoses: moderate esophagitis, chronic gastritis, problems with bacterial infections.

Later, doctors began to focus on a new diagnosis: autoimmune enteropathy. It is a rare disorder, a catch-all term to describe unexplained problems with the digestive tract. They struggled to explain how the surgery caused it or triggered it, or how they missed it in screening.

Still in Pain

By September, the Hardys returned home to North Carolina. Still in pain and nauseous, Ashley began her sophomore year in high school going half-days. In January, she began going full time. Her stomach pain tends to taper off as the day wears on. She still is being fed protein formula through a stomach tube each night.

"Does she live with pain? Yes," said Ashley's mother. "Will she always live with pain? Yes. I don't think this kid will ever live without pain."

Ashley, now 16, said she had lost 130 pounds since the operation. She weighs 235. She would like to lose another 30. Her sleep apnea is gone. She can move around with greater ease.

"As for the surgery, what can I say? It did its purpose. It helped me be more healthful. It helped me lose weight. It has certainly been quite an ordeal," said Ashley, the rasp in her voice now gone.

ELEVEN

Plastic Surgery Can Improve Body Image

Robert A. Ersek

In this article, originally appearing in *Cosmetic Surgery Times*, internationally acclaimed plastic surgeon Robert A. Ersek defends the multiple liposuction procedures and tummy tucks that he performed on a twelve-year-old girl. He explains that he decided to perform the procedures because the girl was both psychologically and physically mature and had been on every diet imaginable beginning from age three with no lasting results, and additionally, her father was dying of cancer. After the procedures the girl continued to lose weight, in part, Ersek explains, because the type of fat that he removed decreases insulin needs, which in turn decreases appetite.

Cosmetic surgery for teenagers may be the fastest growing segment of cosmetic surgery, but it is not without controversy. I recently had a 12-year-old patient from whom I removed 33 pounds of fat . . . by liposuction and on whom, a few months later, I performed an abdominoplasty [surgery that reduces the area of the stomach].

A local newspaper ran a Sunday front-page story on the little girl, which resulted in *People* magazine and a host of other media outlets carrying it.

Robert A. Ersek, "First Person Surgical, Pre-Teen Procedures: How Young Is Too Young for Lipo and Tummy Tuck?" *Cosmetic Surgery Times*, vol. 10, March 2007, pp. 44–47. Copyrighted publication of Advanstar Communications Inc. All rights reserved. Reproduced by permission.

Professional Blow-Back

Much to my surprise, I received a great deal of criticism and hostility from many quarters. The circumstances around this case are quite unusual, but the bottom line is that I had been called upon to justify my position of performing liposuction and an abdominoplasty on a youngster. Some thought the physical make-up was just too immature to consider something so life changing

Brooke Bates, believed to be the youngest American to have liposuction surgery, is thrilled with her new body.

as cosmetic surgery. Others thought that the risks of any surgery were just too great to be considered for a teenager. One nationally recognized plastic surgeon flatly stated that teenagers should not run to their plastic surgeon—they should just run.

Psychologic Maturity

I am not certain at what point in the chronological passing of time psychological maturity occurs. Certainly some children who live in a very protected environment with little social interaction remain immature into their 20s or perhaps their whole life. Others seem to be quite gregarious and quite sensible at a very early age. As such, every case should be taken individually. I do not think there can be a specific rule of exactly what age is "reasonable." I have delivered babies for a few girls at age 11 and plenty at 12 or 13. Psychological maturity is certainly a sliding scale.

Physiologic Maturity

Some of the criticism has been based on the simple fact that surgery is risky and even riskier in a young person. I am unaware of any studies showing that younger people heal more slowly than older people or that younger people are less resistant to complications of surgery than older people.

In fact, recent studies have been performed with surgery in utero because the very youngest seem to heal the very best. When earthquakes and other disasters have occurred, often the survivors that last the longest in the most traumatic situations are the youngest.

A Special Case

In this particular case, there were extenuating circumstances. The patient was 12 years old when we first met. Her father called and asked if I would consider liposuction for his 12-year-old daughter.

Initially, I said, "No. She should consider diet and exercise." Well, her dad had been a patient of mine for about 25 years. He said, "This girl weighs 225 pounds and is at her wit's end." To which I responded, "At age 12, people can grow out of things and she should get on a serious diet and exercise regimen."

He told me that she had been dieting and exercising since age three and that her life was miserable.

"The kids make fun of her. She tries to run at school but she is so heavy that she gets red in the face. The school has asked us to make her stop running in school because they think she will faint. We have tried everything we can think of. Please just talk to her."

The Patient's Perspective

The patient came in with her mother and father and explained that she had been dieting and exercising her entire life. Her mother was very insistent that she had tried everything: Deal-A-Meal, Weight Watchers, liquid protein diets, starvation diets and exercise to the point of exhaustion. She would lose a few pounds and then a few weeks later she would gain it back plus a little more.

I explained that often children are chubby. My own daughter was chubby but grew out of it. Her mother stated that the girl's doctor told them that she was prediabetic and that she just had to lose the weight. They did not know of a way this could be done with the usual behavior modification methods.

I suggested gastric bypass or a lap band. One of their neighbors had recently died from a gastric bypass, so they felt that option was out of the question. I explained that we could remove a safe amount of fat (5 or 10 liters), wait six weeks and take another 5 or 10 liters, and wait six weeks and then do another 5 or 10 liters. In other words, we could do this in an outpatient setting a little bit at a time. They were very anxious to get started on the program.

Extenuating Circumstances

On one visit, while her father was not with them, the patient and mother explained that they would like to proceed more quickly than the multi-year program I had outlined because Dad was on chemotherapy for metastatic bladder cancer. He was losing weight, on high doses of steroids, and his appearance was getting worse by the week. The daughter said, "I would like my dad to see me in a dress before he dies."

Her panus [fat overhang] was very large and redundant and therefore no amount of liposuction would cure that. However, because of their temporal considerations, I agreed to remove a maximum amount of fat by liposuction in one session if she donated two units of blood to herself ahead of time. Then, a minimum of six weeks later, assuming she had fully recovered with no complications, we would perform an abdominoplasty. Again, because she had such a large panus, I did not perform any liposuction in that area.

Surgical Steps

At surgery, we first infiltrated Xylocaine with epinephrine. The infiltration was about 8 liters. Fifteen liters total aspirate was removed. At the end of the procedure, we gave her the two units of autologous [her own] blood. We used blunt cannulas [tubes] that have a maximum of 6 ml with a blunt tip and blunt holes. We have cannulas that are 45 ml in length. All of this was done through simple stab incision in the buttocks crease, two small incisions in the pubis, and one behind each ear where a 3-ml blunt cannula was passed. The procedure was all done under Valium and ketamine dissociative sedation and she went home the same day. Her postoperative course was uneventful; she missed one week of school.

A Metabolic Defense

At about two months, we proceeded with the abdominoplasty. The patient had been 219 pounds on our scales and was down to 190 pounds prior to abdominoplasty. When last seen in our office two weeks ago, she weighed 155 pounds.

In addition to the critical questions that we received following the publication of this case, Gerard Illouz, who has done liposuction longer than anyone, sent me a very nice letter complementing the patient on the success of this operation.

Sharon Giese, who wrote the definitive paper with Scott Spear regarding Metabolic Modulation believes, as I do, that removing large amounts of subcutaneous fat decreases appetite insulin needs, circulating blood sugar, and systolic blood pressure and also has a long-lasting effect of appetite suppression. We have seen several patients who have lost tremendous amounts of body weight after a modest amount of liposuction. One went from a size 10 to a size 2, another from a size 14 to a size 4.

One of our most carefully studied patients had gestational diabetes and took her fasting blood sugar every Monday morning for years. Her blood sugar was always between 150 and 200. After removing 10.2 liters of fat by liposuction, her blood sugar dropped to 100 and has stayed there for several years. She had always dieted and exercised and controlled her weight to some extent, but after liposuction, she lost an additional 60 pounds over the next 6 months. Giese called to tell me that she believed that we had saved this girl's life and either prevented or postponed the onset of type 2 diabetes.

We have begun a practice of recording fasting blood sugar and/or hemoglobin A1C (an index of glucose levels over three months) for all of our overweight patients. In many cases, what is considered a high normal hemoglobin A1C of 5, 6 or 7 is significantly reduced following liposuction, although it is not true in every case. We have had body builders for whom we did liposuction in whom the hemoglobin A1C increased three months after surgery.

Questions and Recommendations

The questions remain, however, how much fat is safe to remove by liposuction with autologous blood provisions and how young can a patient be? It is my considered medical opinion that age is not a sole factor. Certainly, we repair cleft lip, ventricular septal defects, and atrial septal defects at an early age. In this patient's case, she had already reached her menarche [first menstruation] and studies by her family doctor showed that her epiphyses had sealed. Although she was only 12 (she turned 13 shortly after the last surgery), she was quite mature and sensible for her age.

In terms of safety, I would not consider or recommend doing liposuction or abdominoplasty under general anesthesia because it carries such a high degree of morbidity and mortality. However, since it can be done under a local anesthesia with Valium

Liposuction Surgeries Performed on Teens (Age 13–19) by Year, 2001–2005

Year	Number Performed	Change from Previous Year
2005	3084	−5 percent
2004	3250	+8 percent
2003	3017	+1 percent
2002	3002	+9 percent
2001	2755	—

Taken from: American Society of Plastic Surgeons.

and ketamine sedation, I believe these procedures are safe and can be performed at any age when indicated.

Obviously, this should be a family decision, and I would prefer to do serial suction over a period of months. But if faced with extenuating circumstances as I've described here, I would not hesitate to act.

We do not advocate that every teenager who wants to lose 2 inches or 2 pounds in order to make the cheerleading squad come in for surgery. However, liposuction, abdominoplasty and other cosmetic procedures can play a critical role in restoring children to normal. Cosmetic surgery, when done under local anesthesia as an outpatient, can safely contribute to the restoration of these children to normal. Liposuction may be the definitive treatment for obesity at any age because the fat is removed. It is an amputation and does not return.

TWELVE

Plastic Surgery Victimizes Women

Sheila Jeffreys

Arena, a British men's style magazine, ran this article, which is an excerpt from a book by Sheila Jeffreys, a researcher and lecturer in politics at the University of Melbourne. Jeffreys takes a bold and unapologetic stance against plastic surgery, suggesting that it meets the criteria of the United Nations' (UN) definition of harmful cultural and traditional practices just as female genital mutilation does. To argue her point she discusses the origin of breast implants, the ill effects of implants, and the link between implants and higher depression and suicide rates. While acknowledging the growing public acceptance and rate of such surgeries, she maintains that the procedures are nothing more than torturous mutilation done merely to gratify men's sexual fantasies.

According to United Nations documents such as the 'Fact Sheet on Harmful Traditional Practices', harmful cultural/ traditional practices are understood to be damaging to the health of women and girls, to be performed for men's benefit, to create stereotyped roles for the sexes and to be justified by tradition. This concept provides a good lens through which to examine practices that are harmful to women in the west—such as beauty practices. But western practices have not been included in the

Sheila Jeffreys, "Beauty and Misogyny," *Arena Magazine*, August 2005, pp. 46–49. Copyright © 2005 Arena Printing and Publications Pty. Ltd. Reproduced by permission.

definition or understood in international feminist politics as harmful in these ways. Indeed there is a pronounced western bias in the selection of practices to fit the category such that only one western practice, violence against women, is included. The implication is that western cultures do not have harmful practices such as female genital mutilation that should cause concern. I argue that western beauty practices from make-up to labiaplasty [genital surgery] do fit the criteria and should be included within UN understandings. The great usefulness of this approach is that it does not depend on notions of individual choice; it recognises that the attitudes that underlie harmful cultural practices have coercive power and that they can and should be changed.

Socially Approved Self-Injury

Changing attitudes and practices will not be easy, however, particularly given the normalisation of cosmetic surgery. For example, according to Elizabeth Haiken in her book *Venus Envy*, between 1982 and 1992, the percentage of people in the US who approved of cosmetic surgery increased by 50 per cent and the percentage who disapproved decreased by 66 per cent. Cosmetic surgery, she says, began at the same time in the US as the phenomenon of beauty pageants and the development of the beauty industry in the 1920s. Haiken points out that cosmetic surgery can be seen as an indication of the failure of feminist attempts to dismantle male domination: 'Cosmetic surgery', she argues, 'has remained a growth industry because, in greater numbers, American women gave up on shaping that entity called "society" and instead turned to the scalpel as the most sensible, effective response to the physical manifestations of age'. Cosmetic surgery, as Haiken points out, was always about putting women into the beauty norms of a sexist and racist society. Women who did not fit American norms had to cut up. Thus by the mid-century, 'Jewish and Italian teenage girls were getting nose jobs as high school graduation presents'.

Breast augmentation, however, is more recent than other types of cosmetic surgery and dates from the early 1960s. This places its origins in the so-called sexual revolution in which men's practice

Breast Augmentation Surgeries

Year	Number of Surgeries	Overview
2006	329,000	Over an eleven-year
2005	291,000	period, more than
2004	264,041	2,300,000 such
2003	254,140	surgeries have
2002	236,888	been performed
2001	219,883	in the United States.
2000	212,500	The number has
1999	167,318	increased each year,
1998	132,387	a trend that seems
1997	122,285	likely to continue.
1996	87,704	

Taken from: American Society of Plastic Surgeons.

of buying women in prostitution was destigmatised through the ideology of sexual liberalism. The sex industry expanded swiftly in the US through pornography and stripping. Breast augmentation was associated in the beginning with 'topless dancers and Las Vegas showgirls'. The method of enlarging breasts for men's pornographic delight in this early period was silicone injections rather than implants. Strippers, Haiken tells us, were getting a pint of silicone injected into each breast through weekly injections. The origin of the practice lay in the prostitution industry created in post-war Japan to service US soldiers who found Japanese women too small for their taste: 'Japanese cosmetologists pioneered the use of silicone . . . after such solutions as goats' milk and paraffin were found wanting'.

The effects on the health of victims of this harmful cultural practice were very severe. The silicone 'tended to migrate'. It could turn up in lymph nodes and other parts of the body, or form lumps that would mask the detection of cancer. As Haiken comments: 'At worst, then, silicone injections could result in amputation, and at the very least all recipients were expected to have "pendulous breasts" by the time they were forty'. In 1975 it was reported that 'surgeons suspected that more than twelve thousand women had received silicone injections in Las Vegas alone; more than a hundred women a year were seeking help for conditions ranging from discoloration to gangrene that developed anywhere from one to fourteen years later'. Silicone implants replaced injections but concerns about the health effects caused the American Food and Drug Administration to impose an almost total ban in April 1992. [The ban was lifted in 2006.] Women who received implants regularly lost sensation in their nipples after the surgery and suffered problems such as encapsulation when scar tissue rendered the breasts hard. Saline implants were favoured where silicone was outlawed. Nonetheless, by 1995, when *Glamour* magazine asked men, 'If it were painless, safe, and free, would you encourage your wife or girlfriend to get breast implants?', 55 per cent said yes. This figure does indicate where the pressure for women to have implants originates.

Breast Implants and Depression

One impulse that underlies women's pursuit of breast implant surgery may be depression. Several studies have shown that there is an unusually high suicide rate among those who have implants. A 2003 Finnish study found that the rate was three times higher than the general population. There is controversy as to the reason for this high rate. Some researchers say it indicates that women who have implants are already depressed and have a tendency towards suicide. The high rate would then suggest that the surgery does not cure the depression. Others say that the suicides may relate to the degree of pain and anxiety women suffer because of the implants. Either way, the suicide rate suggests that breast implants are not positively correlated with women's mental health. . . .

Midriff Mutilation

The body types featured in sexual entertainment spawn other forms of extreme mutilation of women. The hipster pants fashion, particularly as portrayed by Britney Spears, has led to a surge in lipo-surgery to create Britney-style flat stomachs. [The

Australian fashion magazine] *NW* features a woman who undertook the nine-hour operation, costing thousands of dollars, because she was 'so embarrassed by her belly'. The patient, Hilary Coritore, explains: 'I'd just like to feel proud of my figure, but right now I'm so ashamed of my belly—it just hangs there. Britney Spears has an amazing stomach, and I'd give anything to look like that. She wears all those low pants and I just wish I could have a stomach as flat as hers.'

In the operation, she receives liposuction to her thighs and upper abdomen to help 'show off' the tummy tuck that took place as

Hao Lulu has implants checked by a doctor before undergoing more than sixteen surgeries to redo nearly every part of her body.

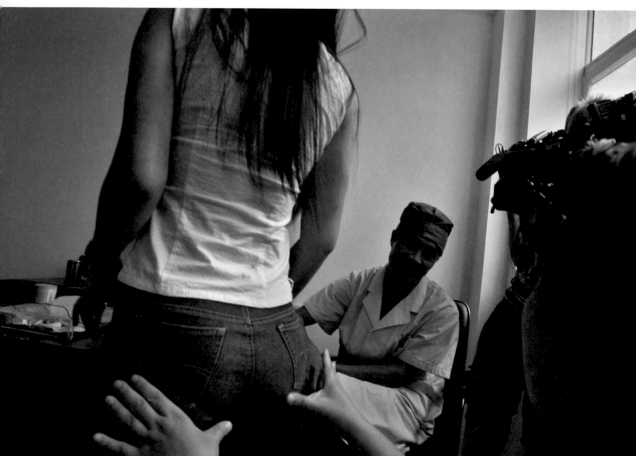

follows: 'A large 15cm-square slice of Hilary's belly is then cut off and thrown away. The whole area from Hilary's pubic bone up to her navel has been removed'. She received breast implants at the same time to utilise the same incision. Cosmetic surgeons like to give the impression that they perform these mutilations for the sake of the women rather than to exploit women's low self-esteem to line their pockets. The surgeon in Coritore's operation says that 'all my girls' in the compulsory 'before' photograph of their almost naked bodies look 'shy, timid and insecure,' but, 'the change I see in my patients in just a few days is so amazing'.

Cosmetic surgeons seem to like to surgically construct their wives, as advertisements for their business, and, presumably, because they then have their favoured fetish objects easily available in their homes. One such is Ox Bismarchi who, according to *NW*, cut up his wife, Brazilian model Angela Bismarchi, ten times in two years. He encouraged her to undertake more surgery and carried it out himself. He says 'When I look at her, I see my own creation.' He is twenty-five years older than this twenty-eight-year-old wife. He gave her 'Pamela Anderson-like breast, a tiny waist and a totally flat stomach' as well as placing 'non-absorbent gels' in his wife's 'calves, lips and cheeks'. He even gave her a dimple in her chin.

The cosmetic surgery carried out on women in the malestream entertainment industry is directed towards making them conform to men's sexual fantasies in order to earn their subsistence. In extreme forms women are made into freaks who cannot physically support the weight of their own breasts and whose faces are contorted masks, but the purpose is related to the dictates of the sexual corvée [duty]. The women are mutilated to provide feasts for men's eyes.

A Savage Practice

The forms of mutilation that are socially approved because they make women more sexually attractive to men—cosmetic surgery and some forms of piercing and tattooing—are usually separated out from the wave of self-mutilations of more extreme or unusual varieties involved in body modification. It is not clear to me that they should be, however. The seriously invasive surgery involved in breast implantation, for instance, would be considered savage if it was carried out at a body modification convention. When it is done by surgeons in the name of relieving supposedly ordinary distress of women about their appearance it can be seen as unremarkable. The connection between amputee identity disorder and cosmetic surgery is usefully made by Dan Edelman who asks 'When in both cases the language used implies a sense of Otherness with respect to one's body, wherein lies the difference in the decision to remove a "foreign" limb versus tucking the tummy or lifting the face of a body that is not a "home"?'

In the face of an epidemic in the west of increasingly severe forms of self-mutilation, it may be time to ask how the attacks on the body may be stopped. The fashion, beauty, pornography and medical industries that justify and promote these forms of self-harm are parasitic on the damage male dominant western societies enact on women and girls and vulnerable constituencies of boys and men.

THIRTEEN

Positive Body Image Comes from Within

Julie Mehta

> Julie Mehta, a writer and editor, wrote this article for *Current Health 2*, a publication for use in middle and high school classrooms. Mehta speaks encouragingly about body image to teens, reminding them that images of stars are always digitally retouched before they grace the cover of a magazine, sometimes radically. So, argues Mehta, it does not make sense for teens to compare themselves with something that is not even real to begin with. She also adds that the definition of beauty varies among cultures and eras and even social groups. Furthermore, she says self-esteem and body image have more to do with how teens think about themselves than how they look and that other people do not really notice what we think are glaring flaws.

A sultry blond stares back from [a] magazine ad, her miniskirt revealing long, slender legs. An underwear model looms large on a billboard, flaunting his six-pack abs. A rock star sprawls across a CD cover, a belly-button ring decorating her toned stomach.

And then there's you. You pass a mirror and glance at your image. What do you see? Maybe there's a zit on your forehead.

Julie Mehta, "Pretty Unreal: Ever Wish You Could Look as Hot as Celebrities Do? Well, They Don't Look as Good as You Think," *Current Health 2*, vol. 31, January 2005, pp. 15–19. Copyright © 2005 Weekly Reader Corp. Reproduced by permission.

Maybe the jeans that fit great last week now feel snug. You've heard it before: Nobody's perfect.

What's a person to think? Perfect images of perfect celebrities are everywhere. It's enough to make anyone feel insecure or envious. "The media sets up impossible comparisons. Whether you're watching sitcoms or music videos or looking through magazines, the images you're seeing are airbrushed and enhanced," said Shari Graydon, author of *In Your Face: The Culture of Beauty and You*. "And research shows that the more time kids spend with image-based media, the worse they feel about themselves."

Falling Short

Seeing all those artificially perfected images can hurt your body image—the way you see and feel about your body and the way you think others see you. From cartoon characters to movie stars, you have probably been exposed to messages about what is considered attractive as far back as you can remember. Those messages can seriously mess with your body image.

"I think the media has a big impact," 16-year-old Erika, of Scottsdale, Ariz., told *Current Health*. "It sets the standard—says thin is in. If the media wasn't saying skinny is appropriate, people wouldn't feel like they need to be so thin." According to Graydon, wanting to be thinner is a huge issue for many girls, while boys feel increasing pressure to be more buff. Boys look at singers such as Usher and realize they'll never have those abs—or the screaming female fans that go with them. In extreme cases, girls develop eating disorders and boys turn to steroids in an effort to achieve an ideal that isn't real.

"It's All Fake"

Celebrities and models are in the business of looking good, and they get a lot of help. Many follow special diets, and others have personal trainers who work with them for several hours a day. Just because they look fit doesn't mean they're healthy, though. Extreme diets can cause health problems, and compulsive workouts can lead to injury.

An ad campaign selling Dove beauty products features "real" women, not models.

Despite models' best efforts, many still don't look "good enough" for the industry. "One hundred percent of fashion photos are retouched," said Brad Adams, a New York City photographer whose retouching service works with advertising agencies. "Usually the eyes and teeth are whitened, makeup and skin problems corrected, and hair cleaned up. Models are already thin, but I've done jobs where even skinny models are made to look skinnier."

Movie stars also receive the "digital diet" treatment, says a woman at another New York retouching service. "Even celebrity snapshots like those in *People*—the paparazzi shots—are retouched. "She explains that Photoshop, a widely used software program, can digitally narrow hips or add to cleavage and make almost any change look realistic. "It's all fake," she added. "Nobody really has skin like that. All human beings have pores and get zits, and once they get rid of those, they have wrinkles."

Pursuit of Perfection

Why is everything touched up these days? "Magazines are supported by ads, and ads are about selling you a product," said author Jessica Weiner, who travels the country speaking to middle school and high school students about body image. "If you feel good about yourself, how many products will you buy? So [advertisers] have to make you feel like you need what they're selling by using unrealistic images." On a more basic level, the woman from the New York retouching company points out, "people like flawless and perfect images."

What, exactly, is perfection? "Different cultures and times define beauty differently," said Graydon. "In North America, large breasts are popular. But in Brazil, [women] get plastic surgery to have smaller breasts and bigger butts. And in Uganda and Peru,

Love Your Body

For the price of:	You could have:
Breast implant surgery	A year of college tuition
A year's worth of Slim-Fast	Plane tickets to Europe
One month of fake tanning	A one-hour massage
A set of salon highlights	Two weeks of groceries
A pair of designer jeans	A lift ticket at a ski resort
A set of acrylic nails	A day at an amusement park
A breast-enhancing bra	An afternoon canoe trip
Twelve fashion magazines	Dinner at a nice restaurant
Another tube of lipstick	A long distance call to a friend

Taken from: National Organization for Women, "Love Your Body Day." loveyourbody.nowfoundation.org.
Reproduced by permission.

heavier women are seen as beautiful." Even in this country, ideals of beauty have shifted widely from generation to generation, from the voluptuous Marilyn Monroe in the 1950s to the waif-thin Kate Moss in the 1990s.

Ripple Effect

Perhaps you don't care what the media say you should look like. Still, you may be indirectly influenced by it through friends and family. "A lot of girls that I know always complain about their bodies," said Ashley, 14, of Wallingford, Conn. "It drives me crazy when they compare themselves to other people that they see in school or on TV."

Family members can also be culprits. If they constantly diet or pump up, you may follow their example—especially if they are concerned about your weight. "A lot of parents have gone through being teased and don't want their kids to go through that," said Kimber Bishop-Yanke, who runs self-esteem camps for girls in Detroit. "I see parents who are concerned their kids are getting fat, but it's normal to eat more and gain weight during puberty. It's just part of growing up."

Mirror, Mirror on the Wall

Of course, no one said growing up is easy. "I'm not fat, but I'm not skinny either," said 13-year-old Jordan, a seventh grader from Baton Rouge, La. "I think I have big thighs, and when I wear shorts they stick out. A lot of kids tease me, but I try not to care so much."

Girls seem particularly prone to body-image issues. "When I was younger, it was harder because I wanted to fit in so much," admitted Natalie, 17, of Humphrey, Neb. Erika from Scottsdale added, "I'm in cheer, and most of my friends want to lose weight." She says she has dieted before and goes to the gym several times a week. Meanwhile, her classmate, Aliraza, 15, says he has never really worried about his looks. "I'm pretty sure girls have a lot more pressure when it comes to appearance."

Tim, a 14-year-old from New York City, agrees there is less pressure on boys than girls but says, "There is still some pressure

—to be more buff." Experts, such as Roberto Olivardia, are starting to pay more attention to the effects of media pressure on boys. Olivardia, an instructor at Harvard University, cowrote the book *The Adonis Complex: The Secret Crisis of Male Body Obsession*, which details a disorder among men that the authors call "bigorexia." Considered the reverse of anorexia, bigorexia occurs when a guy sees himself as puny no matter how muscular he is. Symptoms may include excessive time spent working out, constant grooming and mirror checking, and anabolic steroid use.

Bigorexia is one type of body dysmorphic disorder (BDD), a medical condition that equally affects males and females. BDD is an ongoing obsession with some small or imaginary problem with one's body. About one of every 50 people suffers from the condition.

Being True to You

Ultimately, body image has a lot more to do with your mind than your body. Self-esteem plays a huge role in body image, so the better you feel about yourself, the more likely it is you'll like what you see in the mirror. Whether you're slim or curvy, lanky or big, the keys to looking your best are eating right, exercising regularly, and feeling good inside.

"You're not your nose or butt or hair on a good or bad day," said Graydon. As a practical matter, most people are way too distracted by their own imperfections to focus on yours, she added. What it all comes down to is that your body is your home for life. Given enough time, you may look back and laugh at the way you once fixated on your body's "flaws."

Natalie couldn't agree more. "As you get older, you get to be more comfortable with who you are, and you learn to be happy with yourself." Why not start by loving your body—and yourself —now?

What You Should Know About Body Image

What Body Image Is
- The way you see yourself
- How you feel about your body
- Part of your self-esteem
- The mental picture you have of your body
- What you imagine other people see and think about your body

Facts About Body Image
- More than 70 percent of all fourth-grade girls report that they are dieting.
- Seventy percent of sixth-grade girls surveyed report that they first became concerned about their weight between the ages of nine and eleven.
- One in four female college-aged women has an eating disorder.
- More than half of all women overestimate their body size.
- In the United States alone, about 10 million girls and women have anorexia and/or bulimia.
- Anorexia is the most fatal psychiatric disorder.
- Twenty-five million people in the United States battle binge-eating disorder.
- If store mannequins were human, they would be too thin to menstruate.

- If Barbie were human, she would have to walk on all fours because of her body proportions.
- Fifty percent of high school-aged boys want a more muscular upper body.
- Seven percent of twelfth-grade boys have used steroids to become more muscular.
- In the United States alone about 1 million boys and men have anorexia and/or bulimia.
- If GI Joe were human, his biceps would be larger than any body-builder in history.

Psychological Disorders Related to Body Image

- *Anorexia nervosa* is a psychiatric disorder in which the irrational fear of being obese results in dramatic weight loss (15 percent of original weight or more). Self-starvation is seen as acceptable, and sufferers can have a distorted image of their bodies, believing they are overweight when, in fact, they are emaciated.
- *Binge-eating disorder* is a psychiatric disorder in which a person at times uncontrollably eats large amounts of food.
- *Bulimia nervosa* is binge-eating disorder, followed by actions to rid the body of calories, most commonly by self-induced vomiting but also by misusing laxatives, fasting, or exercising excessively.
- *Body dysmorphic disorder* is a psychiatric disorder in which a person is preoccupied with an imagined or minor physical defect or defects.

Signs of Anorexia and Bulimia

- Physical
  - Rapid weight loss or gain
  - Feeling cold all the time
  - Dry hair or skin, dehydration, blue hands/feet
  - Lanugo (fine body hair)
  - Calluses or bruises on knuckles; light bruising on eyelids, under the eyes, and on the face or neck
  - Loss of menstrual cycles
  - Dizziness and headaches

- Behavioral
  - Dieting or chaotic food intake
  - Pretending to eat; throwing away food
  - Exercising for long periods of time
  - Constantly talking about food
  - Frequent trips to the bathroom
  - Wearing baggy clothes to hide a very thin body
- Emotional
  - Mood swings, tiredness, and depression
  - Complaints about appearance, particularly about being or feeling fat
  - Sadness or comments about feeling worthless
  - Perfectionist attitude

Signs of Steroid Abuse

- Acne
- Increased appetite
- Overdeveloped upper-body muscles
- Needle marks over large muscle areas
- Mood swings and aggressive behavior ("roid rage")
- Deepened voice (for women)
- Hair loss resembling male-pattern baldness

What You Should Do About Body Image

If you had a magic wish, what would you do with it? The number one secret wish of girls eleven to seventeen is to be thinner. The body that more than half of all eleven- to seventeen-year-old boys would choose for themselves, if possible, is attainable only through steroids. Is this normal? There is nothing wrong with taking good care of your body and making it the best that it can be, and part of being a teenager is creating your identity and being very conscious about how you look. However, a huge gap exists between the television and magazine images and what is normal—to the point that finding normal is not so easy. So how can you know what is normal? What should you do about the problem we all seem to be having with body image?

Understand the Human Body

The human body has limitations. For most people, looking like the latest top model is as impossible as growing six inches taller —or shrinking six inches. There is not one ideal weight for your height. Your body type, muscle mass, and bone structure have a lot to do with your family history. Yes, you can lose weight and add muscle, but only to a certain extent, and for some people even that is less attainable than for others. Also understand that weight and fitness are two separate things; in fact, muscle weighs more than fat.

Understand the Media

The images of thin women and muscular men that fill our heads after watching television or a movie, looking at billboards, or browsing the magazine aisle are human ideals. In fact, those images are so ideal that most of them are not even naturally attainable. Photos on billboards, in magazines, and even movies are often airbrushed. Extreme muscles are often the result of chemicals that will eventually destroy other parts of the body. Corporations use advertising images to sell products.

Examine Your Own Body Image

Listen to how you talk to yourself about your body. Are you constantly comparing yourself with other people? Do not focus on others; focus on yourself. Strive for your own personal best, not someone else's. Do you talk negatively to yourself about your body? Do not say things to yourself that you would not dare say to your best friend because they are so mean. Be your own best friend. If you are having trouble knowing what you say to yourself about your body, try writing in a journal, reading a book about body image, or talking to someone.

Love Your Own Body

Do not think of your body as the enemy, but as something valuable that you love and take care of. Do not put yourself on a harsh diet, but eat nourishing foods. Do not think of exercise as punishment, but as play—your own personal recess or recess with friends. Instead of spending money on diet pills, diet magazines, or diet programs, spend it on something nurturing like a massage, free weights, or a great water bottle. Realize that starving, purging, or injecting harmful chemicals into yourself is as self-destructive, if not more self-destructive, than smoking, taking illegal drugs, or binge eating. Focus on how you feel and how your clothes fit instead of how much you weigh.

Examine the Way You View and Treat Others

Making assumptions about a person based upon their physical appearance is no different than making assumptions about people based on their sex, race, or nationality. "Fat-ism" is no better than classism, sexism, or racism. Start by talking positively about your own body instead of putting it down. Be aware of how people around you talk about their own bodies and other people's bodies. Challenge their assumptions as well as your own. Speak up when family members make fun of other people's bodies for whatever reason. Do not worship other people's bodies, either.

Gravitate toward people who respect and nurture their bodies. Body hate is contagious.

Take a Stand

Loving your own body and speaking up to people that you see every day is a good start. You can also raise awareness in other ways. Tape positive messages on a mirror, even your own mirror. Create and post signs in your school to create awareness about body image issues. Use stickers to label ads that you think promote eating disorders. You can post the ads or send them to the company responsible for them in protest. You can also write letters. About-Face has a directory of corporation addresses and also posts letters that their Web site visitors have written to corporations, along with responses to the letters. Start a campaign at your school.

ORGANIZATIONS TO CONTACT

About-Face
PO Box 77665, San Francisco, CA 94107
(415) 436-0212
e-mail: info@about-face.org
Web site: www.about-face.org

About-Face's mission is to equip women and girls with tools to understand and resist the stereotypes of women the media disseminates. The three components to About-Face's program, Education into Action, are media-literacy workshops, action groups, and a resource-filled Web site. Its workshops and action groups reach throughout the San Francisco Bay Area.

Academy for Eating Disorders (AED)
111 Deer Lake Rd., Ste. 100, Deerfield, IL 60015
(847) 498-4274
fax: (847) 480-9282
e-mail: info@aedweb.org
Web site: www.aedweb.org

The AED is a global, multidisciplinary professional organization that provides professional training and education; inspires new developments in eating disorders research, prevention, and clinical treatments; and is an international source for information in the field of eating disorders. Through its Web site AED provides free online access to the full text of a number of articles from the *International Journal of Eating Disorders*, an AED publication.

The Body Positive
PO Box 7801, Berkeley, CA 94707
(510) 528-0101
fax: (510) 558-0979
e-mail: info@thebodypositive.org
Web site: www.thebodypositive.org

The Body Positive promotes the Health at Every Size (HAES) health model, which encourages people of all sizes to adopt healthy lifestyles by becoming physically active; consuming nutritious foods; developing healthy eating attitudes and habits; and developing social support, self-respect, and positive body image.

Do Something
(212) 254-2390
e-mail: www.dosomething.org/contact
Web site: www.dosomething.org

Do Something believes young people have the power to make a difference. The organization seeks to inspire, support, and celebrate a generation of doers: people who see the need to do something, believe in their ability to get it done, and then take action.

Girlshealth.gov
8270 Willow Oaks Corporate Dr., Ste. 301, Fairfax, VA 22031
e-mail: http://girlshealth.gov/contact/form/index.cfm
Web site: www.girlshealth.gov

The mission of the Girlshealth.gov Web site, developed by the Office on Women's Health in the Department of Health and Human Services, is to promote healthy, positive behaviors in girls between the ages of ten and sixteen. The site gives girls reliable, useful information on the health issues they will face as they become young women and tips on handling relationships with family and friends, at school and at home.

KidsHealth
e-mail: https://secure02.kidshealth.org/parent/kh_misc/send_mail.html
Web site: www.kidshealth.org

KidsHealth provides doctor-approved health information about children from before birth through adolescence. Created by the Nemours Foundation's Center for Children's Health Media, KidsHealth provides families with accurate, up-to-date, and jargon-free health information.

Mind on the Media

710 St. Olaf Ave., Ste. 200, Northfield, MN 55057

(952) 210-1625

fax: (866) 623-1464

e-mail: tbio@mindonthemedia.org

Web site: www.mindonthemedia.org

Mind on the Media is an independent organization focused on raising public awareness about the negative effects of images in the media. Mind on the Media does not take part in any political activities like supporting or opposing candidates for public office or lobbying for the passage or defeat of legislation, but develops educational activities regarding media literacy.

National Association to Advance Fat Acceptance (NAAFA)

PO Box 22510, Oakland, CA 94609

(916) 558-6880

e-mail pr@naafa.org

Web site: www.naafa.org

NAAFA is a nonprofit human rights organization dedicated to improving the quality of life for fat people. NAAFA has been working since 1969 to eliminate discrimination based on body size and provide fat people with the tools for self-empowerment through public education, advocacy, and member support.

National Association of Anorexia Nervosa and Associated Disorders (ANAD)

PO Box 7, Highland Park, IL 60035

(847) 831-3438

e-mail: anadhelp@anad.org

Web site: www.anad.org

ANAD is a nonprofit corporation that seeks to alleviate the problems of eating disorders, especially anorexia nervosa and bulimia nervosa, by educating the general public and health-care professionals, encouraging and providing research, and acting as a resource center.

National Eating Disorders Association (NEDA)
603 Stewart St., Ste. 803, Seattle, WA 98101
(206) 382-3587
toll-free: (800) 931-2237
e-mail: info@NationalEatingDisorders.org
Web site: www.nationaleatingdisorders.org

NEDA is the largest not-for-profit organization in the United States working to prevent eating disorders and provide treatment referrals to those suffering from anorexia, bulimia, and binge eating disorder and those concerned with body image and weight issues.

National Institute on Drug Abuse (NIDA)
6001 Executive Blvd., Bethesda, MD 20892-9561
(301) 443-1124
e-Mail: information@nida.nih.gov
Web site: www.steroidabuse.gov

NIDA is part of the National Institutes of Health (NIH), the principal biomedical and behavioral research agency of the U.S. government. NIH is a component of the U.S. Department of Health and Human Services. NIDA has authored Steroidabuse .gov, which provides links to information and resources about anabolic steroid abuse.

National Institute on Media and the Family
606 24th Ave. S., Ste. 606, Minneapolis, MN 55454
(612) 672-5437 or (888) 672-KIDS
fax: (612) 672-4113
e-mail: www.mediafamily.org/about/contact.shtml
Web site: www.mediafamily.org

Since 1996, the National Institute on Media and the Family has worked to help parents and communities "watch what our kids watch." This research-based organization reports on the positive and harmful effects of media on children and youth, providing editorial and informational articles as well as family activities online.

National Mental Health Information Center
(800) 789-2647
Web site: www.mentalhealth.samhsa.gov

The Substance Abuse and Mental Health Services Administration's (SAMHSA) National Mental Health Information Center provides information about mental health via a toll-free telephone number, a Web site, and more than six hundred publications. The National Mental Health Information Center was developed for users of mental health services and their families, the general public, policy makers, providers, and the media.

National Women's Health Information Center
(800) 994-9662 • TDD: (888) 220-5446
e-mail: www.4woman.gov/contact/index.cfm?sawquestions=yes
Web site: www.4woman.gov

The National Women's Health Information Center is an information Web site sponsored by the Office on Women's Health (OWH), which was established in 1991 within the U.S. Department of Health and Human Services. Its vision is to ensure that "all women and girls are healthier and have a better sense of well-being." Its mission is to "provide leadership to promote health equity for women and girls through sex/gender-specific approaches." The strategy OWH uses to achieve its mission and vision is through the development of innovative programs, by educating health professionals, and motivating behavior change in consumers through the dissemination of health information. Fact sheets, reports, and a "Teen Survival Guide" are all available through the Web site.

Overeaters Anonymous
World Service Office
PO Box 44020, Rio Rancho, NM 87174-4020
(505) 891-2664
fax: (505) 891-4320
e-mail: info@oa.org
Web site: www.oa.org

Overeaters Anonymous is a fellowship of individuals who, through shared experience, strength, and hope, are recovering from compulsive overeating. The organization welcomes anyone who wants to stop eating compulsively. Members of Overeaters Anonymous may be extremely overweight, moderately overweight, average weight, underweight, still maintaining periodic control over their eating behavior, or totally unable to control their compulsive eating.

Weight Control Information Network
1 WIN Way, Bethesda, MD 20892-3665
(202) 828-1025 or (877) 946-4627
fax: (202) 828-1028
e-mail: win@info.niddk.nih.gov
Web site: www.win.niddk.nih.gov

The Weight Control Information Network (WIN) is an information service of the National Institute of Diabetes and Digestive and Kidney Diseases (NIDDK), National Institutes of Health (NIH). WIN was established in 1994 to provide the general public, health professionals, the media, and Congress with up-to-date, science-based information on obesity, weight control, physical activity, and related nutritional issues. WIN also developed the *Sisters Together: Move More, Eat Better* national initiative to encourage black women to maintain a healthy weight by becoming more physically active and eating healthier foods.

BIBLIOGRAPHY

Books

Audrey D. Brashich, *All Made Up: A Girl's Guide to Seeing Through Celebrity Hype and Celebrating Real Beauty*. New York: Walker, 2006.

Leslie Goldman, *Locker Room Diaries*. Cambridge, MA: Da Capo, 2007.

Sheila Jeffreys, *Beauty and Misogyny: Harmful Cultural Practices in the West*. New York: Routledge, 2005.

Autumn Libal, *Can I Change the Way I Look?* Broomall, PA: Mason Crest, 2005.

Courtney E. Martin, *Perfect Girls, Starving Daughters: The Frightening New Normalcy of Hating Your Body*. New York: Simon & Schuster, 2007.

Robyn McGee, *Hungry for More*. Emeryville, CA: Seal, 2005.

Valerie Rainon McManuns, *A Look in the Mirror*. Washington, DC: Child & Family, 2004.

Tamra B. Orr, *When the Mirror Lies*. New York: Franklin Watts, 2007.

Samantha Schoech, *The Bigger the Better, the Tighter the Sweater: 21 Funny Women on Beauty, Body Image, and Other Hazards of Being Female*. Emeryville, CA: Seal, 2007.

Periodicals

William Lee Adams, "Amputee Wannabes," *Psychology Today*, July/August 2007.

Jerry Adler, "Toxic Strength," *Newsweek*, December 20, 2004.

Nancy Alfaro, "The Myth of the Perfect Body," *Dance Magazine*, July 2006.

Stephanie Armour, "Your Appearance, Good or Bad, Can Affect the Size of Your Paycheck," *USA Today*, July 20, 2005.

Laura Hensley Choate, "Counseling Adolescent Girls for Body Image Resilience: Strategies for School Counselors," *Professional School Counseling*, February 2007.

Hilary de Vries, "Why We're at War with Our Bodies," *Marie Claire*, July 2006.

Marilyn Elias, "Race Doesn't Reflect on Women's Poor Body Image," *USA Today*, July 25, 2006.

Carl Elliott, "Putting Your Best Face Forward," *Psychology Today*, May/June 2004.

Andrea Faiad, "Your Body, Yourself: You Don't Have to Be Perfect to Like the Way You Look," *Current Health 2*, March 2006.

Carlin Flora, "The Beguiling Truth About Beauty," *Psychology Today*, May/June 2006.

Latisha Forster-Scott, "Sociological Factors Affecting Childhood Obesity: Culture Plays a Role in People's Attitudes Toward Exercise, Nutrition, and Body Image," *Journal of Physical Education, Recreation and Dance*, October 2007.

Adriane Fugh-Berman, "Cosmetic Mutilation? Shameless Self-Confidence!" *Women's Health Activist*, July/August 2004.

Christina Gillhaim, "More than Push-Ups: Kids and Fitness," *Newsweek*, June 18, 2007.

Robin Givhan, "Rounding Off Their Figures: For Women of Color, a Fuller Beauty Standard," *Washington Post*, February 16, 2007.

Harvard Reviews of Health News, "Gastric Bypass for Teens," August 2, 2006.

Danylo Hawaleshka, "I Hate My Fat Legs," *Maclean's*, December 19, 2005.

Nanci Hellmich, "Do Thin Models Warp Girls' Body Image?" *USA Today*, September 26, 2006.

Michael Hill, "Experts: Male Eating Disorders Climbing," *Tucson Citizen*, May 12, 2004.

Theresa Howard, "Ad Campaigns Tell Women to Celebrate Who They Are," *USA Today*, July 8, 2005.

Kristen Kemp, "Special Report: Weighing In," *Girls' Life*, June/July 2006.

Linda H. Lamb, "Feel-Good Body Image Studio Aims to Ease the Weight of the World," *State*, August 1, 2005.

Colleen Long, "Fashion Magazines Showing More Body Types," *Kearney Hub*, August 9, 2005.

Frederick N. Lukash, "Plastic Surgery, Teenagers, and the Media," *Plastic Surgery Products*, June 2007.

Hara Estroff Marano, "The Skinny Sweepstakes," *Psychology Today*, February 2008.

Medical Ethics Advisor, "Should Surgery Be an Option for Obese Adolescents?" March 2004.

Julie Mehta, "Body Myths," *Current Health 1*, March 2005.

Michelle Meyer and Bevin Cummings, "In Fine Form: Meet Three Women Who—After Years of Struggle—Realized They Already Had the Bodies They'd Been Looking For," *Real Simple*, August 1, 2004.

Lois B. Morris, "Healthy Body Image: It's Never Too Early to Start Building One," *Prevention*, June 2005.

Leah Paolos, "The Language of Fat: Are You Constantly Criticizing Your Body? Discover How Those Negative Words Are Masking Your True Feelings, and Learn How to Express Yourself More Honestly," *Scholastic Choices*, April/May 2006.

D'Anna Piro, "Adolescent Girls' Body Perceptions as a Result of Sport Participation," *Journal of Physical Education, Recreation and Dance*, February 2007.

Katherine Presnell, Sarah Kate Bearman, and Mary Clare Madeley, "Body Dissatisfaction in Adolescent Females and Males: Risk and Resilience," *Prevention Researcher*, September 2007.

Monica Rizzo, "I Like My Curves!" *People Weekly*, June 11, 2007.

Nicholas A. Roes, "Body Image a Critical Factor in Treatment of Adolescent Girls," *Addiction Professional*, July 2005.

Geneen Roth, "Getting Past Size-Zero Envy: You Can't Resist the Lie That 'Thin Equals Happy' Without Help," *Prevention*, October 2005.

———, "Looking at Real Women's Bodies Will Help You Learn to Love Yours," *Prevention*, August 2004.

Sandy Fertman Ryan, "About Face," *Girls' Life*, February/March 2005.

———, "Love That Bod! Do You Have a Case of Bad Bod-itude? Lose It . . . by Feeling Beautiful from the Inside Out," *Girls' Life*, June/July 2005.

Michael Smith, "Genes, More than Fashion, Induce Anorexia," *Medpage Today*, March 6, 2006.

Mark R. Sultan, "When Plastic Surgeons Say No," *USA Today*, May 2005.

Michelle Tackla, "Beautiful Minds?" *Dermatology Times*, September 2003.

Floris Tomasini, "Exploring Ethical Justification for Self-Demand Amputation," *Ethics & Medicine*, Summer 2006.

Peg Tyre, "Fighting Anorexia: No One to Blame," *Newsweek*, December 5, 2005.

US Newswire, "Body Image Has Little Influence on Desire for Plastic Surgery, ASPS Study Reveals," October 18, 2007.

———, "Childhood Obesity and Liposuction Are Not a Good Mix, ASPS Cautions," April 4, 2007.

———, "New Study Shows Surgical Treatment on Breast Asymmetry Improves Quality of Life," December 17, 2007.

———, "Some Patients Stop Needing Antidepressant Medication After Having Plastic Surgery; Study Presented at American Society of Plastic Surgeons Annual Meeting," October 8, 2007.

————, "Surgeons Find That Laparoscopic Banding Procedure Helps Overweight Adolescents Lose Weight and Improve Health," October 8, 2007.

Jessica Weiner, "The Language of Fat," *Cosmo Girl*, February 2006.

Kirsten Weir, "Fat Chance: Lawrence Capici Had Radical Surgery to Lose Weight. Should Other Obese Teens Follow His Example?" *Current Science*, January 7, 2005.

————, "Limb and Life: Life Goes On After Limb Loss," *Current Health 2*, February 2007.

Ashley Williams, "One Teen's Gastric Surgery," *People Weekly*, December 17, 2007.

Eric Wilson, "Health Guidelines Suggested for Models," *New York Times*, January 6, 2007.

INDEX

PICTURE CREDITS

AP Images, 6, 7, 12, 18, 21, 29, 32, 46, 50, 56, 63, 70, 80, 85
Bob Riha Jr/WireImage/Getty Images, 40,
Steve Zmina, 10, 15, 23, 26, 37, 45, 53, 59, 65, 75, 78, 86